Love's Conquest

Georgie Sheldon

In the interest of creating a more extensive selection of rare historical book reprints, we have chosen to reproduce this title even though it may possibly have occasional imperfections such as missing and blurred pages, missing text, poor pictures, markings, dark backgrounds and other reproduction issues beyond our control. Because this work is culturally important, we have made it available as a part of our commitment to protecting, preserving and promoting the world's literature. Thank you for your understanding.

LOVE'S CONQUEST
Sequel to
HELEN'S VICTORY

By MRS. GEORGIE SHELDON

AUTHOR OF

"Nora," "Trixy," "Brownie's Triumph,"
"Earle Wayne's Nobility," "A
True Aristocrat," Etc.

i.e. Sarah Elizabeth Forbush Downs

A. L. BURT COMPANY
PUBLISHERS   NEW YORK

Copyright, 1900
By STREET & SMITH

LOVE'S CONQUEST

CHAPTER I.

A GAY PARTY IN PARIS.

AND now, while Helen and her dear invalid are resting and recuperating their wasted energies, after their long months of gloom and trial, we will transfer our readers across the Atlantic to a charming villa just on the outskirts of Paris, which Mrs. Ellsworth and her sister, Mrs. Sturdyvant, had occupied for several months, and where they had kept open house during that time, entertaining many of their countrymen and women, as well as distinguished people of other lands.

Thus they, together with Marjorie, had led a charming life throughout the winter and they were very loath to leave gay, delightful Paris, in spite of the fact that they were looking forward to a very enjoyable summer, for they had arranged to join a party of tourists, who were going to Norway and Sweden, and afterward make an extended tour of the Continent.

On entering this elegant abode, as we are privileged to do, we find a charming and social company seated at dinner, and learn, from their conversation, that they comprise the very people who are going upon the trip already referred to.

It is the last day of May, and Mrs. Ellsworth has

gathered them together to talk over the last few arrangements that must be made before they leave, which they intend to do within the coming week.

Everybody appears to be in the best of spirits, and impatiently anticipating the flitting, unless we except Rob, our hero, who still looks somewhat pale, and appears much graver than when we last saw him.

He had never seemed quite the same happy, carefree young man since he received that—to him—inexplicable letter from Helen, the fatal decree of which had swept over him like a blighting wind, withering all his fondest anticipations.

From that hour there had also grown upon him a gravity and reserve that was wholly unnatural to him, and, with this change, there had seemed to arise a barrier between his uncle and himself, and which was a source of much anxiety and regret to the elder gentleman.

Mr. Lancaster strove to overcome this strained and abnormal condition of things by every means in his power, but in vain.

Rob was invariably courteous and was dutifully attentive to his wishes as ever. He was agreeable when they were by themselves, and made an effort to be cheerful and entertaining when they were out among their friends; he did not sulk, or make his grief conspicuous; nevertheless, there was an unmistakable constraint in his manner that was a continual reproach to Mr. Lancaster.

He seemed to have locked away, as if in a tomb, his secret sorrow and disappointment—to have shut up his heart, and barred its door, and his doting uncle missed, more than he could express, his former boyish frankness and confidence, for heretofore he had never failed to discuss freely with him whatever arose to perplex or harass him.

He knew that the young man could have no suspicion of the part he had borne in causing the misunderstanding and break with Helen; no one, save Hubert Alton himself, as he fondly believed, shared that secret, and he had not the slightest fear that it would ever be revealed.

Nevertheless, he had reasons for hating and despising himself—as if he had been a reprobate third party —for what he had done, while, at the same time, he invariably justified himself for having saved Rob from rashly ruining his own life.

Still, he was troubled and uneasy about the boy; he had taken the matter so much more to heart than he had anticipated; he had grown thin; he often looked so pale, harassed, and ennuied, although no word of complaint ever escaped his lips, that he was at his wits' end to know how to arouse him to his former energy and vivacity and interest in life.

With the hope of effecting this, he had persistently dragged him into society all winter long; he had sought the gayest scenes and people, joined parties upon excursions on every point of interest, and, in fact, spared nothing which his fertile mind could suggest or money accomplish to tempt him to forget.

It was with this end in view, added to the fact that Hubert Alton had not yet succeeded in carrying out the scheme they had planned before he left America, that he had decided to remain abroad for another year, and join a party of tourists who contemplated traveling extensively.

Rob had demurred when the plan was first broached to him, but Mr. Lancaster—feeling that it would be very unwise to allow him to return, in his present mood, to New York, where he would be liable to meet Helen, when explanations might ensue, and their former relations renewed—was insistent, and the young man quietly yielded the point.

They had been constant visitors at Mrs. Ellsworth's

pretty villa ever since they had come to Paris. In fact, the three ladies of the household had spared no pains to make them feel that their house was a kind of home for them, and their success in these endeavors was very satisfactory, at least to Marjorie and her mother, both of whom—although neither had ever breathed the thought to the other—had the same project in view.

Upon his first meeting with her, at St. Moritz, Mr. Lancaster had instinctively shrunk from renewing his acquaintance with Mrs. Ellsworth, who had been somewhat unpleasantly associated with some disagreeable experiences of his early life. But she had met him so charmingly and affably; she had referred— once only—to that unpleasant episode, frankly and regretfully, blaming herself for having allowed herself to become involved in the affair, that he was disarmed, and was inclined to feel that she might, after all, have been the victim of circumstances that had made her an unwilling participant in the affair.

She continued to play her cards very cleverly, and, in time, completely won his confidence and gratitude by her kindness to him and Rob, while Marjorie, after her arrival, having taken his heart entirely by storm with her beauty, her childlike innocence and trust, he found an additional charm in their household, which gradually became the most attractive place in the world to him for the time being.

Both Mrs. Ellsworth and Mrs. Sturdyvant were cultivated ladies. They were exceedingly well read, and took great pains to keep abreast with the times in art, literature, and music, as well as in current events; thus they made themselves very companionable and entertaining.

They also drew about them people no less brilliant and refined; while, keeping "open house" as they did, their home could not fail to be a most delightful rendezvous to all who were so fortunate as to be welcomed within its portals.

Mrs. Ellsworth, as has already been intimated, had been left in very comfortable circumstances, and being a good manager, she knew how to make the most of every dollar; thus she was thought to be richer than she was, and this added to her prestige wherever she went.

Mrs. Sturdyvant was also a widow of considerable fortune, consequently, as she had no children of her own, Marjorie's prospects, as far as worldly expectations were concerned, appeared to be very flattering.

So, with the girl's manifest fondness for him, and his for her, there gradually grew up in Mr. Lancaster's mind the plan to effect a union between her and Rob, if he could manage it, hence his visits to the villa were, perhaps, more frequent than they might otherwise have been, and also his readiness, when approached on the subject by Mrs. Ellsworth, to join the tourist party.

As may have been surmised, the scheming woman was the projector of the tour, and had planned it for the very purpose of throwing Rob and Marjorie more closely together, hoping thus to bring about the match she coveted.

There were four other young people in the party, two sisters by the name of Barton, with their parents, a Mr. and Mrs. Welling, with their son and a ward of Mr. Welling's—a young man of twenty, who had inherited a considerable fortune.

The Misses Barton were exceptionally nice girls, but quiet and ordinary, and thus Mrs. Ellsworth had no fear of having Marjorie's charms eclipsed, while, as for the other young men, she knew that the girl cared nothing for them.

But, to return to the dinner party at the villa. When the meal was over the company adjourned to the drawing-room, to continue the discussion of their plans, while the dining-room was being cleared for dancing, some other guests having been invited to participate in the festivities of the evening.

A small but fine orchestra had been provided for the occasion, and, ere long, music and mirth were at their height.

Rob felt obliged to participate in the merry-making, although his heart was not in it, and he would have much preferred to steal away for a quiet smoke and a reverie by himself, but he could not do this without appearing rude and selfish, for there were fewer gentlemen than ladies present, and he knew that he would be expected to do duty among the dancers.

"Robbie, what makes you so glum to-night?" Marjorie playfully demanded, as they paused to rest a moment, during a waltz which he had begged of her.

The girl was always full of mischievous and pretty mannerisms, and now and then she would lapse into a freedom of speech as above, although generally she addressed him demurely as "Mr. Eggleston."

He smiled amusedly down upon her laughing, upturned face, much as he would have done upon a sportive child, for she seemed more like a child than a woman to him.

"'Glum!' Is it possible that I appear like that in the midst of this brilliant and charming company?" he queried.

"Indeed you do," she retorted, with a pretty pout and a decidedly reproving nod. "I don't believe you have really smiled—naturally—once this evening. All during dinner you sat like a grave and dignified professor, who was absorbed in some abtruse theme with which he proposed to astonish his colleagues the next time he appeared among them."

"Really, Miss Marjorie, I did not dream that I was drawing down upon my humble self such critical observation," Rob returned, flushing slightly, but trying to speak lightly.

Marjorie lifted an appealing glance to him.

"Truly, R—Mr. Eggleston, I—I wish you wouldn't be quite so high and mighty—so shut in upon yourself," she said coaxingly. "I had told the Misses Barton how very nice you are——"

"Thanks, awfully," interposed the young man, and laughing out "naturally" for the first time that evening.

"Well, but you are nice, when you choose to be," she persisted; " and I want them to think well of you—especially as we are to be compagnons de voyage for so long. And, besides——"

She broke off suddenly, dropping her eyes, with a pretty air of embarrassment.

"And, besides what, little Miss Monitor?" demanded her companion, and regarding her admiringly, for she was particularly lovely that evening, in a fairy-like robe of pink mousseline de soie made over pink silk, with roses of the same color, and maiden-hair fern for garniture.

"Well," she said, with a soft sigh, but toying nervously with her fan, "it makes me afraid that you are unhappy over something, and keeping it to yourself—you have seemed so for a long time—and—it hurts me. I like to have everybody around me happy."

"I believe you do, Marjorie," Rob responded, with unusual gentleness, but with paling lips, for he was more unhappy than any one had any idea of. He was touched, too, by her discernment of his mental condition, and the sympathy which her words and manner betrayed. "Well, little girl," he added, after a moment, and forcing himself to speak more cheerily, "I will endeavor, from this time on to deserve the high praise you have bestowed upon me—I will try to be 'very nice.' Now, shall we resume our waltz?" and he slipped his arm again about her waist.

But she held back, and lifted an earnest look to him.

"Why do you speak like that to me?" she inquired gravely. "Do I seem like a 'little girl' to you?"

Again Rob laughed out.

"Do you object to the term?" he questioned. "Why, I often hear Uncle Hal call you that."

"Oh, well, I like to be 'little girl' to him," she said naively, and with significant emphasis. "It seems so fatherly in him to say it to me, and I have always so longed for a father, you know. But—with you, it is different; it—seems to put such a—distance between us, and—I am not so very much younger than you, if I am not six feet tall," she concluded, with a saucy nod of her bright head, which came exactly to his shoulder.

"The fates forbid!" retorted Rob, as he ran an appreciative eye over her pretty, symmetrical figure. "I would not add a single inch to your height—it would mar the proportions, in my opinion. No, Petite, we all like you best just as you are; but I won't call you 'little girl' again, if you do not like it," he smilingly concluded, as he swung her out upon the floor, and they resumed their interrupted waltz.

If he had only said "I like you best just as you are," Marjorie would have been in the seventh heaven of delight, but, because he had generalized the remark, her heart sank heavily, for she felt that she was not gaining ground with him at all.

He was always courteous and kind in his manner toward her, and so was every one else, for that matter, for it was the acknowledged fact that she was the pet of the whole circle of their acquaintance. Indeed, Marjorie always made friends wherever she went— with the women, as well as with the men—"for, she shrewdly reasoned, "one gets on so much nicer in the world to have everybody fond of one."

Presently, hoping to entice Rob into resuming their confidential conversation, she remarked that it was very warm, and suggested that they go out upon the veranda for a few minutes.

"All right," he readily responded. "Uncle Hal is out there. I will take you out, and find you a seat by him, but I am engaged for the next dance to one of your friends, the elder Miss Barton, and," with a significant laugh, "I feel it incumbent upon myself to redeem my character and prove, if possible, the truth of your assertions regarding your honorable servant."

Marjorie was disappointed not to be able to continue her tete-a-tete with him, but she concealed the fact, and suffered herself to be taken out to Mr. Lancaster, who had slipped away to have a quiet smoke in the moonlight on the porch. His nerves had recently received something of a shock, and he wanted a chance to think.

"Here is a young lady whom I am going to leave in your care for a while, Uncle Hal," Rob observed, as he moved a chair to the gentleman's side. "She has found it very warm inside, and, as I have duties in another quarter, I am unable to remain to entertain her."

"All right, Rob," smilingly returned the gentleman, and involuntarily putting out his hand to Marjorie, who confidingly laid hers within it; "we are always good friends, are we not, Petite? And enjoy a chat by ourselves. Sit down my rose-colored fairy," touching her dress caressingly, for he was fond of gay colors, "and talk to me, for I believe I have an attack of the blues to-night."

" 'Et tu, Brute?' " quoted Marjorie, with a roguish laugh, as she sank into a chair beside him.

"What especial signification has that quotation to

my remark, my child?" her companion inquired, and regarding her curiously; "aren't you happy to-night?"

"Oh, yes; I am always happy," she said brightly, "but Rob isn't, evidently. I've just been calling him to account for being so absent-minded and grave to-night."

"Is he? I have not observed him particularly," said Mr. Lancaster indifferently, as he removed his cigar, and flicked the ashes from it with his little finger, and then he immediately fell into a brown study again.

Marjorie sat quietly by him for a few moments, wondering what could have caused his unusual mood.

Then, her curiosity becoming piqued, she remarked insinuatingly:

"I hope you have not had bad news to-day, Mr. Lancaster?"

CHAPTER II.

MRS. ELLSWORTH'S DISCOVERY.

THE man started violently at her question, for he had lost himself, and entirely forgotten her presence.

"What an unsocial old chap you must think me, little girl, and I beg your pardon for being so rude!" he exclaimed, sitting erect, and giving himself an impatient shake. "Bad news?" he continued; "well, I have had news recently, and which is not altogether a surprise to me, and I am somewhat in doubt whether to regard the intelligence as good or bad," he contincluded, with a doubtful intonation and a gleam in his eyes, which told of a mind ill at ease.

"Ah!" said Marjorie in an inviting tone.

"Yes; one of my clerks, in New York, is about to be married," Mr. Lancaster volunteered.

"And—and is going to marry some one of whom you do not approve?"

"Well, I cannot say that, exactly, for I know that his fiancée is a most estimable young lady, although I am not personally acquainted with her. I have simply been wondering if the marriage will prove to be a happy one, for I am quite sure that the young man is far her inferior—in some respects, at least," the gentleman explained. "By the way," he added, with sudden thought, "I have heard you speak of her occasionally—her name is Helen Seymour. She is going to marry one of my assistant bookkeepers. Hubert Alton, on Saturday—to-morrow—at twelve o'clock."

Marjorie never moved, to betray the slightest surprise at this astounding information.

At the same time, she felt as if she had been suddenly galvanized; for a keen, tingling sensation pervaded her every nerve, almost forcing a cry of pain from her lips.

It was the most amazing thing she had ever known, she thought, that fate should have played so completely into her hands; for, without the slightest authority or reason, she had been using Hubert Alton's name in connection with Helen's for months, for the sole purpose of making Rob jealous, and estranging the lovers.

She had never, for a moment, dreamed that Helen could be won from her allegiance to the young man, for she believed her to be made of too loyal fiber ever to give her hand to another while her heart belonged to Rob, and she was just dying to learn more about the affair.

But she would not have betrayed either curiosity or ignorance for anything. She was not going to allow Mr. Lancaster to imagine that she had been kept in the dark regarding the movements of her friend.

"Why!" she exclaimed in well-assumed surprise; "is Hubert Alton a clerk in your employ? Helen has often mentioned him in her letters to me, but she never happened to tell me that he was in your office. Well, it was but a natural sequence to their friendship, I suppose, although I did not know that the date had been set. Helen has not replied to my last letter, but I shall probably have one in a day or two."

"Then, you correspond with her regularly?" observed Mr. Lancaster inquiringly.

"Yes," was the barefaced falsehood, for she had not heard from Helen for months, although she had pretended that she had. "What a sly puss she has been not to have written me before this of her plans!" she went on glibly; "I shall scold her well for it, for, of course, I should have liked to send her something handsome for a wedding present. I am sorry, though," she added gravely, "that you do not think Mr. Alton quite her equal; and—do you know"— with a covert glance at the gentleman's face, which she could see distinctly in the moonlight—"I used to think, when I saw so much of her last summer in the Adirondacks, that she was rather fond of R—Mr. Eggleston. She used to have a good deal to say about him; she has a fine picture of him, too, and would blush every time his name was mentioned."

"Ah!" said Mr. Lancaster, in a non-committal tone. Then he added, with more of interest: "You think Miss Seymour is rather a fine young lady, I believe?"

"Yes, indeed; I think she is just lovely!" enthusiastically responded Marjorie, who felt inspired to do Helen full justice, now that she had been—or was about to be—swept out of her path. "She is one of your honest, high-minded girls, who would not do a wrong or mean thing to save her life. She is beautiful to look at, too; she is sweet-tempered, and absolutely fascinating in manner—everybody was wild over her last year—and as unselfish as the day is long. If"—with a regretful sigh—"I could be as good, as pure, and lovable as Helen Seymour, I should feel that I was pretty sure of—well, of heaven."

Mr. Lancaster's heart sank heavily within him as he listened to this high praise of the fair girl against whose happiness he had been plotting.

Ever since receiving and responding to Hubert Alton's telegram, giving the date of his proposed marriage with Helen, he had been oppressed with a sense of guilt, not only on account of the part he had played toward Rob and the girl he loved, but also because of the ignoble temptation to evil that he had placed in Hubert's path.

He had regretted the act almost from the hour he had committed himself, for he had then suffered a shock to his self-respect from which he knew he would be long in recovering, if, indeed, he ever could regard himself as an honorable gentleman again.

"Well," he remarked, with a slight smile, "she certainly has one ardent admirer; but, possibly"—with an uneasy shrug—"in your fondness for her, you may somewhat overestimate her attractions and worth?"

"No, indeed," said Marjorie positively. "I am sure that any one who knows her would tell you the same. Why Rob has met her, you know, and he, too, thinks she is lovely. By the way, what does he say about her marrying Mr. Alton?" she inquired in conclusion, with a rapidly beating heart.

"Could the news of this union have caused Rob's unhappiness and abstraction to-night?" she asked herself.

"I—have not said anything regarding the matter to him," her companion returned.

His tone was quiet and matter-of-fact; but something in his manner and the slight hesitation in his reply told Marjorie a great deal.

She was shrewd, and she surmised, at once, that there had been a serious passage-at-arms between the uncle and nephew about the relations of the latter with Helen. Yes, she even began to suspect that he had been brought abroad to get him away from her influence, for she could see that the high-toned Mr. Lancaster was ambitious for his prospective heir, and would wish him to choose a wife from his own circle in life.

And she could understand, also, that, if they had ever had words upon the matter, Mr. Lancaster would shrink from agitating a subject that was fraught with discord between them by announcing Helen's marriage to Hubert Alton.

Just at this point, Marjorie adroitly changed the subject, and it was not referred to again; but the pretty schemer mapped out a course for herself to pursue, while she chattered, and which she devoutly hoped would bring matters to a propitious crisis for herself in the near future.

She had no intention of allowing Rob to remain in ignorance of Helen's marriage, his uncle's reticence to the contrary notwithstanding.

This was on Friday evening, at the very hour during which Helen, with a pale face and a heavy heart, was packing her trunks and making ready for the dreaded ordeal and flitting set for the morrow.

On Saturday morning Rob rode out from the city to the villa upon some errand connected with their proposed trip of the coming week.

Marjorie from her chamber window saw him turn into the avenue leading to the house, but she did not go down at once to receive him as usual.

He had been chatting nearly fifteen minutes with Mrs. Ellsworth and Mrs. Sturdyvant when she came tripping into the room, looking like some sweet, guileless fairy in her simple dress of spotless dimity, with knots of blue ribbon tucked here and there about her corsage, and carrying an open letter in her hand.

"Ah! good morning, Mr. Eggleston," she said, lifting a smiling glance of welcome to their visitor. "I hope you will excuse me for not coming down immediately; but I was so interested in my letter I just couldn't leave it until I finished it. See what a long one it is," she went on, shuffling the sheets as she stood beside him, and Rob thrilled to his finger-tips as he recognized the dear, familiar handwriting.

He changed color slightly, and a wistful look burned in his handsome eyes. He would have given half his year's allowance for the privilege of reading that letter by himself.

But he greeted Marjorie courteously, and genially assured her that she was freely pardoned.

"Aunt Eliza," said the artful girl, as she approached Mrs. Sturdyvant, "guess who my letter is from."

The epistle, by the way, was several months old.

"I do not need to guess, dear," said the lady, as she laid a caressing hand upon her arm, "for I know the handwriting. It is from that pretty Miss Seymour whom we met and with whom you were so friendly in the Adirondacks last summer."

"Yes, and such news, auntie;" pursued Marjorie, and seemingly intent only upon what she had to tell— "guess again."

"Well, I should say, judging from your eagerness, there could be but one subject that could arouse you to such a state, and that is marriage," responded Mrs. Sturdyvant, laughing. "Is Miss Seymour really going to be married?"

"Auntie, you are awfully cute!" retorted Marjorie gayly, and shaking the letter at her with a playful air. "Yes, Helen is going to be married, and this very day. Let me see"— turning to glance at the gilded clock on the mantel—"it is now half-past ten here in Paris; at twelve precisely, by New York time, she will become Mrs. Hubert Alton—— Mercy! what has happened?"

She broke off suddenly in the midst of her news, and exclaimed as above, as the sound of crashing glass smote upon her ears.

She wheeled quickly around, to see Rob bending to gather up the pieces of a broken tumbler which his sudden start as he caught the fatal import of Marjorie's words, had dashed from the table beside which he was sitting.

He began to apologize in an incoherent way for the accident, when Mrs. Ellsworth politely interposed.

"Never mind, Mr. Eggleston," she said, as she rang for a servant. "It does not matter in the least. Ninon, remove the broken glass!" she added in French to the maid who appeared.

As Rob resumed his seat the three ladies observed that he had grown very pale; but only one surmised the cause or paid much heed to the fact.

"This is quite a surprise, isn't it, Marjorie? Does your friend give you the particulars regarding her marriage?" questioned Mrs. Ellsworth, who was always interested in a wedding.

"She does not go as fully into details as I wish she had, mamma; there is not much about her trousseau. Helen Seymour is a girl who cares very little for gewgaws and show, compared with your rattle-pated daughter. She has a good deal to say about her mother, who has been very ill, you know—although she is improving. I am not so very much surprised," she went on volubly, to give Rob time to recover himself, for she could see that he was terribly upset— "that she should marry Mr. Alton, although I did not think it would come quite so soon, for she has often mentioned him in her letters, in a way to make me feel pretty sure that their friendship would result in matrimony. By the way, Mr. Eggleston, you once told me that Mr. Alton was a classmate of yours—how old is he?"

"About my own age, I should judge—possibly he may be a year older," Rob replied, and struggling to speak naturally, although he was barely able to hear his own voice for the ringing in his ears.

"Do you think he is worthy of Helen Seymour?" pursued the unfeeling little schemer. "You know, I think her about as near perfection as any human being can be."

"I—I sincerely hope he is, for I too, think she is one of the loveliest girls I ever knew—there are few her equal," Rob returned, with heroic loyalty. "I have

not met Alton, however, since we left the High, so
have known nothing of him personally since then."

He arose as he ceased, for he could bear no more.
His head was in a whirl, his brain seemed on fire, and
his heart like a lump of ice in his bosom.

"Oh, pray do not go," all three ladies protested in
one breath.

"Stay and lunch with us," Mrs. Ellsworth hospitably
added.

"Thanks, I must ask to be excused to-day, and I
shall not see you again, probably, until we start upon
our trip next week, as Uncle Hal and I contemplate
taking a little run into the country for a day or two,"
Rob returned, but he was white even to his lips, and
both Mrs. Ellsworth and Mrs. Sturdyvant thought
he must have been taken suddenly ill and did not
urge him further.

Marjorie, however, knew well enough what troubled
him, and her own heart was in a tumult as she realized
how strong a hold upon his heart Helen had obtained.
She had deliberately planned the scene just described, for the sole purpose of letting him know
that the girl was going to be married and with the
intention of crushing all his hopes in that quarter.
Rob took leave of them, and bowed himself out,
eager to get away by himself, where he could hide
his anguish from every curious eye.

Helen was to be married at noon that day!—and to
Hubert Alton! It seemed utterly incredible to him.
He felt that he could not have it so—his whole
soul arose in rebellion against such a sacrifice, for
he knew that she was far superior to the young
man, and that she could not fail to discover her
mistake when it would be too late to remedy it. He
had been very unhappy—wretched, in fact, ever since
his correspondence and his relations with her had
been broken off, and he now blamed himself severely

for having so tamely submitted to his congé; he felt that he should have written Helen again and demanded her reasons for what she had done. He realized now, that he had never given up the hope of being reunited to her—that he had comforted himself in a measure with the belief that, when he should see her personally on his return, everything would be satisfactorily explained and all would be well again.

But now—ah! it drove him wild to think of it!— Helen was to be married at noon to-day! The words rang in his ears like the knell of doom.

He could scarcely see the road to guide his horse, as he rode back toward the city; a blinding headache had settled upon him and every pulse was beating with the speed of a race-horse. He managed to reach his hotel, where he crept stealthily up to his room and staggered to his bed, upon which he threw himself exhausted with the conflict of emotions within him, and conscious of nothing save his own misery.

Marjorie had followed Rob out as he left the house, and stood watching him from the porch as he rode away.

"It was like plunging a dagger into him," she muttered, with frowning brow and clouded eyes, "but it had to be done or there never would be the slightest chance for me."

"Eliza, who is this Helen Seymour with whom Marjorie is corresponding?" Mrs. Ellsworth inquired, as her daughter left the room. "I've often thought of asking you about her, for she seems to have made a deep impression on Marjorie; but we have been in such a whirl ever since we came to Paris I have neglected to do so."

Mrs. Sturdyvant flushed slightly at her sister-in-law's question, and, for an instant, was at a loss how to answer her. She had promised Mrs. Seymour that she would not betray her identity; but, after meeting Halburton Lancaster, who had been associated with that sad drama of the past, the heart-broken woman's face had haunted her continually, and at intervals all winter long she had been tempted to tell Mrs. Ellsworth of the interview with the wronged friend of her youth, and try to influence her to make what reparation might lay in her power, even though she realized that nothing could ever atone for the long years of sorrow during which she had lived alone and borne the blame of another's sin.

And now, in spite of her pledge, she was impelled anew to reveal the truth, with the hope of arousing her sister's conscience and so bring something of peace and love into the life of that lovely woman who had so appealed to her sympathy just previous to her departure from America.

"Marien," she said, while she searched her face curiously, "Helen Seymour is—Margaret Wilton's daughter."

CHAPTER III.

HELEN'S YOUTH.

MARIEN ELLSWORTH sprang erect in her chair, the elaborate piece of fancy-work which she had been engaged dropping from her nerveless fingers, every particle of color fading out of her handsome face.

"E—liza! Heavens! You cannot mean it! It can't be true!" she gasped.

"It is true, Marien," quietly responded Mrs. Sturdyvant.

"But you told me—you wrote me——"

"Yes, I wrote you last summer, in reply to your inquiries, that I did not know anything about Margaret Wilton—that I had never heard anything of her since—since that awful scrape. That was true at that time. What I learned afterward came as a thunderbolt to me, the same as my revelation has come to you to-day. You know that Marjorie made the acquaintance of Helen Seymour during her visit with me. I had seen the girl a number of times, and thought her lovely, as does every one else who has met her. I had intended to call upon her and her mother, for they were neighbors, and I wished to show my appreciation of Helen's instruction; for Marjorie certainly improved wonderfully during her lessons with her. But I kept putting it off during a day or two before we left for New York. Then I ran over, just at dark, and found Mrs. Seymour alone, fortunately, and the moment she presented herself before me I recognized her, and, for an instant, would have been glad to have had the earth open and swallow me."

"Eliza! You have fairly taken my breath away!" Mrs. Ellsworth exclaimed excitedly. "I—I firmly believed that she was—was dead."

"You would be glad, perhaps, if she had died."

"I—well, I should not have grieved myself to death, if such had been the case," the woman admitted, with a laugh that was almost hysterical; "it—it would have ended everything, you see. So—she married again?"

"No, indeed; she is a heart-broken woman still. Seymour is a name that she assumed to conceal her identity."

"But—but, Helen——"

"Her daughter was born nearly eight months after Margaret disappeared."

"Great heavens! Then she is his child!"

"Yes; that is evident from her resemblance to him, although I had never observed it until after I learned the truth," Mrs. Sturdyvant replied.

"Do you suppose that Hal Lancaster knows that she is living?" questioned Mrs. Ellsworth, with a slight shiver.

"I imagine that he knows nothing whatever about her, and I am sure she would not wish him to know of her existence."

"Why have you never told me this before, Eliza?" demanded Mrs. Ellsworth irritably. "Do you suppose I would have allowed Marjorie to correspond with that girl if I had known?"

"Marjorie may well be proud of having made the acquaintance of Helen Seymour, and grateful for every line that she has written her, for she is honesty, purity, and goodness personified—which is more than can be claimed for my niece, I regret to admit," Mrs. Sturdyvant dryly observed. "Why did I not tell you before?" she went on; "well, as you have said, we have been in such a whirl I have hardly had the opportunity, and then I shrank from reviving those long-past experiences. Besides—I had promised Mrs. Seymour that I would keep her secret—that I would not betray her identity——"

"Then why have you done so now?" interposed Mrs. Ellsworth, with a note of resentment in her tones.

"Well, to tell the truth, Marien, the woman has haunted me all winter, and I pity her from the bottom of my heart. It was easy to see, from her looks and manner, that she has had a desperate struggle in life, and the old wound still bleeds in secret to-day. It seems cruel, wicked, and—if you would only do what is just—confess your agency in that miserable scheme, which resulted so disastrously for her when she was as innocent as a child, that terrible wrong might, perhaps, be made right to a certain extent, even at this late day."

"Eliza Ellsworth Sturdyvant! what are you thinking of? Do you imagine, even for a moment, that I would bend to that? Never!" cried Marien Ellsworth, pale with rage at the suggestion.

"You are only piling up future agony for yourself by refusing to do her justice, when you alone were instrumental in ruining her life—yes, two lives; you will have to meet and answer for it some day," said Mrs. Sturdyvant gravely.

"Nonsense, Eliza!" snapped her companion angrily. "I am looking out for number one in the present. I don't take much stock in future judgments. Besides, Margaret Wilton had no business to keep two men dangling after her."

"She did not; you know that she was true to her husband; loyal to her heart's core to him, and she had no love for the other——"

"Well, but she managed to make that other love

her," was the resentful retort, while a crimson spot burned on each of Mrs Ellsworth's cheeks.

"You know that is not true, either, Marien," said her sister-in-law sternly. "She repulsed him; she did everything to discourage him; but you happened to love him yourself, and you allowed your insane jealousy to spur you on to a mean revenge, hoping if you could ruin the character of your rival and crush her you might win the man for yourself, when you not only incurred his contempt, but also lost your truest friend. I never could understand how your conscience could allow you to do such a deed when you were under such heavy obligations to Margaret."

Mrs. Ellsworth laughed disagreeably.

"Don't you know, Eliza, that people always hate those who have imposed obligations upon them?" she retorted, with an evil smile.

"You are doubly responsible, then, for having accepted her favors," was the severe rejoinder. "Just think of what she did for you that last year you were in school, after your father died? She paid every bill, so that you could remain to graduate; then, as soon as she was married, she took you into her own home and treated you exactly like an own sister; then——"

"Bah! Eliza—don't rehearse all that—don't preach!" interposed Mrs. Ellsworth angrily. "You know I never could tolerate it, and I am not going to begin now. Of course I know that Margaret did a great deal for me, but—there is one thing that a woman can never forget or forgive, and that is winning the affections of the man whom she loves."

"She was not to blame because he loved her——"

"All the same, he did love her; he adored her, and I would have sold my soul for a tithe of what he lavished upon her. But he never forgave me—he would never see me again after that day," said Marien Ellsworth, with trembling lips and a wail of pain in her tones that told its own story.

"Did you imagine you could retain his respect after what you had done?"

"Well, things didn't turn out just as I expected; but Margaret hasn't had all the suffering, Eliza; for since we are discussing these matters, I may as well own that I have never ceased to love him—I love him still!" the woman confessed, with burning cheeks.

"And would you marry him now, if——"

"Indeed I would to-day—this hour, and even go upon my knees to sue for his pardon," the woman vehemently interrupted. "But enough of this for now, Eliza," she went on, with more composure. "Tell me how Margaret looks; where has she been all these years? What has she been doing?"

"One question at a time, if you please, Marien," said her companion, smiling slightly. "'How does she look?' She is a grandly beautiful woman——"

"Oh!—after all her terrible struggles, et cetera?" was the sneering interposition.

"She certainly is," persisted Mrs. Sturdyvant; "she is evidently a woman whose trials have purified and refined her; she shows that in her exquisite face. She is more fully developed than when we last saw her; her figure is perfect; her bearing like that of a queen. If Hal Lancaster and John Wilton could see her as I saw her that day—dressed in pure white, with a touch of lavender here and there, and all her former charms in their perfection, they would be more dead in love with her than ever."

Marien Ellsworth ground her beautiful white teeth together in jealous rage at these encomiums pronounced upon her old-time rival.

"You needn't have thrown that at me, Eliza," she said, under her breath, and referring to her last remark. "Of course I have no means of knowing what John's attitude may be toward her—wherever the man may be—but I don't believe that Hal Lancaster cares a straw for her, after all these years."

"I believe you mean to capture the man yourself; is that your game, Marien?"

Mrs. Ellsworth laughed out defiantly.

"Well, that remains to be seen," she retorted. "He is handsomer than he ever was, and rich enough to tempt an even more ambitious woman than I am. At any rate, I mean that Marjorie shall marry his nephew, if I can bring about the match, by hook or by crook. He will be the heir of his uncle's wealth—if he does not marry himself; he is a fine fellow, too, and I would like nothing better than to have him for a son-in-law."

"And I am sure that Marjorie would echo your sentiments," thoughtfully replied Mrs. Sturdyvant. "It is plain to be seen that she is very fond of him, but——"

"But what?" demanded Marjorie's mother, with some show of resentment.

"I am not sure that she would be the wife best suited to him."

"Now, pray, don't begin to croak again, Eliza," returned Mrs. Ellsworth, with a frown. "I am sure Marjorie is lovely—a dainty little piece of humanity as one cares to see; she is well educated, even talented in some ways, and she makes friends with everybody."

"Yes, I grant all that; but you may as well own the truth, Marien; she does nothing except from selfish motives; she is all self. I love the girl, too; she is my only brother's child, and I expect to leave her all that I possess; nevertheless, I am not blind to her faults. She is unprincipled and untruthful, in spite of her many attractions; but I keep hoping that something will yet arouse her to the fact that 'that way lies destruction,' and cause her to mend her ways. If she was as good and pure and guileless as she appears to strangers, I should simply worship her," Mrs. Sturdyvant concluded, with evident emotion.

"Well, Eliza; you don't gloss anything over for relationship's sake!" was the sharp retort.

Mrs. Ellsworth and her sister-in-law were in the habit of "sparring it" as above, now and then, but would get over the ill feeling that was thus temporarily engendered after awhile, and go on most amicably again, until something else came up upon which they disagreed.

Mrs. Sturdyvant was Mrs. Ellsworth's superior by far, morally, and she would have much preferred to give her brother's widow a wide berth; but she was fond of Marjorie, as she had said, and, having no children of her own, she yearned over the girl with all her motherly heart.

Whenever she had come to visit her she had faithfully striven to inculcate a love of truth and rectitude in her, and while she seemed to inherit some of her father's noble qualities, the worthy woman feared that the lack of principle which had always been a feature of her mother's character would eventually wreck her life.

She had hoped much from her intimacy with Helen Seymour during the previous summer, little dreaming that that lovely maiden was the daughter of the woman whose hopes and happiness Marjorie's mother had ruined twenty years before.

"It seems very strange that Marjorie should have fallen in with that girl, of all persons in the world, last year," observed Mrs. Ellsworth, after a lengthy pause, during which the thoughts of both women had been busy with the past. "And she actually seems to be fond of her. I don't like it," she added, with a frown, "and I shall put an end to their correspondence immediately."

"Then you will deprive your daughter of the purest influence that she has ever known during her life," was the grave response.

"I can't help it—there shall be no intimacy between my family and hers!" was the bitter retort.

"Mercy, Marien! how you must hate that innocent woman! I believe you would not hesitate to do her another lasting injury, even now, were the opportunity offered you. I did not dream that any one could be so cruelly vindictive," said Mrs. Sturdyvant, while she regarded her companion with surprise.

Mrs. Ellsworth laughed out with shrill bitterness.

"It certainly would not be safe for her to cross my path again," she muttered, and, hastily rising, she abruptly left the room.

"Truly, I am afraid that I have made a mistake in telling her that I met Margaret Wilton last summer," Mrs. Sturdyvant murmured regretfully, as the door closed with a violent bang. "I promised her that I would keep her secret; but I pitied her so! Her face and her sad eyes have haunted me ever since, and I thought that, if Marien could be induced to make a full confession, and John Wilton could be reached and persuaded to do what is just and right, she might perhaps have the evening of her life made peaceful and happy. But Marien is as hard as adamant; she will never yield an iota. And to think that she loves him still, and would marry him, if she could, even at this late day! But she evidently feels that that is a lost cause, and so is setting her cap for Mr. Lancaster. I wonder if—— Oh!" suddenly cutting herself short and heaving a long sigh—"what a strange world this is! or, rather, what strange people there are in it!"

Tuesday morning, following the above incidents,

a party of twelve people—six young ladies and gentlemen and as many adults—left Paris under the supervision and guidance of a competent courier en route for Norway and Sweden. All, save two, appeared to be in the best of spirits, and looking forward with the brightest anticipations to their tour. Rob and Mr. Lancaster, however, seemed to be somewhat under the weather, for both were pale and grave and taciturn. Rob looked as if he had had a fit of sickness, since Saturday, for his face was sunken; he was hollow-eyed and he had lost several pounds of flesh.

His uncle was evidently very uneasy on his account, for he watched him incessantly, and, without being intrusive, was attentive to his slightest need.

On Saturday, when he had returned to his hotel to lunch, he had found Rob's door locked, and, as the key had been removed, he concluded that he had been kept at the villa, as was often the case.

When he did not appear at dinner Mr. Lancaster sought him again in his room and this time gained admittance. He was simply appalled—shocked at the change which only a few hours had wrought in his appearance.

"Rob! what is it? You are ill!" he exclaimed, in alarm.

"No, Uncle Hal; I am not physically ill," Rob replied, in a weary tone. "I suppose, though, I might as well tell you the truth—my heart is broken—my life is ruined—for Helen Seymour was married at noon to-day."

Halburton Lancaster was smitten dumb with astonishment and dismay at this unexpected intelligence, and he felt almost like a murderer as he looked into the handsome, despairing face before him and realized that he alone was responsible for the wrecking of his life and happiness.

"How do you know—how did you hear?" he faltered.

"Marjorie Ellsworth had a letter from Helen this morning, telling her of the—the event," replied Rob, repressing a groan of anguish. Then he added, shutting his teeth with a resolute snap: "But go, please—leave me alone and I will fight it out by myself. I can't go into the country to-night, as we planned, but I will be ready to join the party on Tuesday morning, so do not fear."

"But, Rob——"

"Don't, Uncle Hal. I can't bear anything now," Rob interposed, with a look in his eyes that told its own story, and the man turned away and left him without another word, but with a heavy heart and an oppressive sense of guilt that he would have given worlds to be freed from.

CHAPTER IV.

A STARTLING PROPOSITION.

They did not meet again until Tuesday morning at breakfast, for Mr. Lancaster would not intrude upon Rob until he signified a desire to see him, although he took care that his meals were punctually served in his room.

He spent a wretched two days by himself, however, and realized thoroughly that the way of the transgressor is hard.

Rob was calm and self-possessed when he appeared equipped for his journey on Tuesday morning, and greeted his uncle with his habitual courtesy and affection; but his changed appearance smote the man keenly, and he felt that he would gladly have forfeited years of his life if he could have undone the wrong he had done, thus restoring his own self-respect and Rob's old-time buoyancy and confidence in him.

He knew him well enough to feel sure that if he should discover the treacherous part he had played, he would sever every bond between them, start out upon his own account in life, and have nothing more to do with him.

It can easily be seen that he suffered grievously, for he was naturally a high-minded man, and his life, for the most part, had been irreproachable. But there had always been an obstinate, self-willed vein in his make-up, which had caused him—when once his heart was set upon anything—never to yield his point until as in this instance, he accomplished his object, and this characteristic had, now and then, cost him dear.

He had not much fear that Rob would ever learn of his agency in separating him from Helen Seymour, for he believed the affair to be a profound secret between himself and Hubert Alton, who, of course, would find it for his own interest to preserve it inviolate.

At the same time he was conscious that his own knowledge of the fact, and some subtle influence of mind acting upon mind, had produced a barrier between himself and his dear boy which he feared would never be annihilated, and this caused him many a remorseful hour.

Rob assiduously avoided the subject of Helen's marriage, and Mr. Lancaster did not allude to it, and tried, when they joined their party at the station, to shield him from the harrowing comments of their friends, who were also very much exercised over his ill looks.

"Yes, Rob is a trifle under the weather," he would remark, to head off inquiries and save the young man from replying, "but he will be all right again in a few days."

Marjorie was especially tactful just at this time.

She greeted him with a simple "Good morning, Mr. Eggleston," but the look of mingled wonder and sympathy in the gentle eyes which she lifted to him seemed to say: "Something is very wrong with you, my friend—something that I do not understand; but my heart is with you, and I am not going to bother you with any remarks or questions."

And she did not. She held somewhat aloof from him for several days, although she never met his glance without giving him a little friendly nod and a cheery smile.

"She is the most sensible one of the lot," Rob said to himself when, at the end of five days, she had scarcely exchanged a dozen words with him. "She sees that there is something weighing on my mind, and she lets me alone."

But this very avoidance of him created a desire on his part to renew his friendly relations with her, for his own society and voluntary isolation had begun to pall upon him somewhat, and the next morning, when he went up on deck—for the party had crossed the Channel and taken a steamer at Hull for Christiania—he found Marjorie already there, and apparently intent upon watching the sun rise.

He was at her side before she was aware of his presence, so absorbed was she in the brilliant scene before her, and she gave a violent start as he lifted his cap and bade her a smiling "Good morning."

"Oh!" with a quick glance at him, accompanied by a brilliant smile and a flush, "you are better, R—Mr. Eggleston! I am so glad."

Apparently it was a hearty outburst of genuine feeling, and it touched Rob.

"Yes, thank you; I am all right," he returned; but he could not quite conceal the pain which even this indirect allusion to his recent suffering caused him.

Marjorie's keen eyes saw the quiver which swept over his face, and at once began talking about something else—the lovely dawn and its marvelous tints; the wonderful voyage they were having; the grand and beautiful scenery and the fiords and the locks—most wonderful of all, by means of which their vessel almost seemed to climb the mountains!

"Oh! I never dreamed of anything like it!" she exclaimed, with pretty enthusiasm and drawing a long breath of delightful appreciation, while her glance swept the enchanting scene before them. "It has been one continuous panorama of beauty—a veritable trip through fairy-land almost from the start!"

"What a little enthusiast you are, Marjorie!" Rob

exclaimed, in a natural tone, and with the first genuine laugh that had escaped him since leaving Paris.

And, for the moment, he had actually forgotten himself and his troubles, for it seemed to him that nothing could be lovelier than his companion's fair face, with that delicate flush on her cheeks, those innocent but sparkling blue eyes looking so frankly into his, and her charming gesture, as she described, with pretty abandon, what had impressed her thus far on their journey.

"I feel almost as if I had been bewitched," she answered, with a breezy laugh, "it is such a beautiful world!—it is so delightful to be alive! I would like to go sailing, on and on, like this forever."

And so she talked on, making him forget himself more and more, until something of the old light returned to his eyes, a healthful hue to his lips and cheeks, and his reserve vanished beneath the magnetic influence of her sunny presence.

When the breakfast bell rang they looked at each other in surprise.

"Why!" exclaimed Marjorie, as she glanced at her watch, "who would have believed it? Can you come down from the heights to anything so intensely practical and common as breakfast?"

"I believe I can," responded Rob, smiling into her dancing eyes, "for to be honest, I must confess to a very plebeian sense of hunger. Come down, Miss Marjorie, at least temporarily, from your flights and heights, and let me take you below."

He offered her his arm, and they went down to the dinging-saloon together.

Both Mr. Lancaster and Mrs. Ellsworth observed their entrance with a thrill of mingled surprise and pleasure, for Rob looked decidedly brighter, while there was an air of good comradeship between the two that was very encouraging.

After that—the ice once broken—the young man mingled more freely with the company, and—though he spent many a sad hour when alone—bravely tried to conceal his trouble and make himself agreeable to his companions.

For a few days he sought Marjorie's society more than that of the others, and the girl did not attempt to hide her undisguised pleasure in being with him, and lapsed into the habit of addressing him has "Rob" instead of "Mr. Eggleston," as heretofore.

But all at once Rob began to notice that she would start at the sound of his step, and her eyes brighten as he drew near her, that a shy blush would creep up to her temples when he addressed her, and a quiver of some inward emotion would pass over her if he took her hand to assist her down a step or over rough ground, or, in fact, happened to touch her at all.

This state of things set him to thinking.

"It will never do for me to attend her exclusively," he gravely told himself. "I have no right to make her or any one else think that I am learning to care for her particularly. Helen was all in all to me—I love her still, in spite of the fact that I have no longer the right, and no other woman shall ever have her place in my heart."

After that he became more general in his attentions, often attaching himself to one or other other of the Misses Barton, during their side excursions, and sometimes seeking the other ladies of the party. He became quite fond of Mrs. Sturdyvant and, after a few weeks, found himself seeking her companionship in preference to that of any one else.

This change in his attitude, although gradual and by no means marked, was indicative, to shrewd Miss Marjorie and her watchful mother, of a state of indifference to the attractions of the former that was decidedly discouraging to their hopes, to say the least.

Neither confided in the other, for Marjorie neither respected nor trusted her mother, while Mrs. Ellsworth fondly imagined that her daughter had no suspicion of her designs.

But both had made up their minds to capture the heir to Halburton Lancaster's tempting fortune, if possible, and each was working for that end in her own way.

All at once the girl began to droop.

She was not assertively depressed or unhappy, but she grew grave and quiet; her laughter, which had been merriest of all, was seldom heard; she lost color, her appetite failed, her manner was listless, and she became indifferent to all that was going on about her, while she would often wander off by herself and sit gazing absently at nothing.

Mrs. Ellsworth began to manifest considerable anxiety and to talk about consulting a physician. Mrs. Sturdyvant did not have much to say, but she quietly watched her niece, and now and then a skeptical smile would wreathe her lips, as she detected the sly glances which she directed at Rob when he was not observing her.

Mr. Lancaster was fondly solicitous for her, and used many devices to win her back to her former manner and spirit; but he also began to suspect something of how matters were going with her, and he would have been more than glad if he could help them along.

Late one afternoon, while they were stopping at a quaint but charming inn at Mariestad, on Lake Werner, in Sweden, Mr. Lancaster came suddenly upon her, sitting by herself in an isolated corner of a porch overlooking a grand stretch of landscape, but seeing nothing, for she was apparently absorbed in her own somber reflections.

"Well, well! my pet, why are you here all alone, when you should be out sight-seeing with the young folks who have gone to do the village and buy souvenirs?" he exclaimed, while he scanned her pale, sad face curiously.

"Yes, I know," Marjorie indifferently returned, with a gentle sigh, "but I did not care to go, and I am tired of souvenirs."

"Um—I imagined young girls were always eager for such things, and the more they had the better they were pleased," said the gentleman reflectively.

But there was no response from the quiet little figure in the corner. She had dropped into her musing attitude again, and seemed oblivious to his presence.

"Are you ill, little one?" questioned her companion, after a few moments, and with a note of tender solicitude in his tones.

"Oh, no!" but the soft sigh rather belied the words.

"Homesick?"

Marjorie laughed out nervously at the question, and the man did not fail to note the slight catch—something akin to a sob—in her breath.

"I have no home to be homesick for, you know," she responded pathetically.

"True—I had forgotten that," said Mr. Lancaster gravely. "Would you like a home, Marjorie?"

"Indeed I would—oh! so much," she eagerly replied. "It would be so delightful to have some place on earth to call one's own and look forward to going back to; but——"

"But what, pet?"

"Mamma does not care to settle anywhere; she enjoys travel and sight-seeing. The responsibility of a home is irksome to her," this with another sigh.

"Well, then, there remains only one thing for you to do to accomplish your desire," said Mr. Lancaster, assuming a jocose air and tone.

"For me to do?" queried Marjorie in perplexity and with refreshing innocence.

"Yes; you must find the right sweetheart, and then make a home-nest for yourself," was the roguish reply.

"Oh!" and now a burning blush suffused the pale, pretty face beside him. Then the red lips began to quiver pathetically, and the lovely eyes slowly filled with tears.

The gentleman's countenance was very tender as he observed these evidences of emotion.

He reached out one firm, white hand to her.

"What is it, dear?" he questioned gently. "Tell me all about it."

With an impulsive gesture that was full of graceful abandon, Marjorie seized the hand thus extended to her in both of hers, bowed her bright head upon it, and burst into a passion of tears.

"Tut! tut! sweetheart!" exclaimed her astonished companion; "what does this mean? I am sure there must be something very wrong with you! Come, come! pour out your overburdened heart into my sympathetic ears, and let us see if I cannot comfort you a bit."

But Marjorie was very shrewd and wise. She had no intention of wearying him with any lackadaisical or sentimental complaints.

She had touched him, aroused his tenderest sympathies, had awakened his suspicion of some secret sorrow, and now she believed she had only to give him an inkling that Rob was the cause of it all and she would have won a faithful ally to her cause.

As if fate had taken special pains to further her scheme, Rob himself came into view that instant, on his return from the village.

He was alone, and was sauntering along with bowed head and thoughtful mien.

Marjorie gave a violent start, and sprang to her feet in the prettiest state of confusion imaginable.

"Oh!" she cried, in a stifled tone of dismay, "there comes Rob—Mr. Eggleston! He must not see me like this!"

And, with a burning face, the tears still glistening on her golden lashes, she fled precipitately into the house.

"Jerusalem! So that is the trouble, after all!" muttered Mr. Lancaster under his breath, and with genuine astonishment. "Well! well! well! I didn't imagine that matters had gone quite so far, and," with a critical glance at his nephew as he drew nearer, "I wonder what Rob would say if I should tell him? She's a dear little thing; so innocent, confiding, and lovable. She'd make him a charming little wife, and I'd just like to bring it about if I could. I'm deuced fond of her—I would have so liked to have a daughter whom I could have loved and petted to my heart's content. Oh, hum! I wonder why my life could not have been more like that of other men—it might have been. I suppose, but for that—damned early mistake," he concluded, with a frown and a heavy sigh, which plainly betokened a heartache of long standing.

"Well, Rob," he continued, addressing his nephew as he mounted the steps and approached him, "what of your sight-seeing, and what has become of the rest of the party?"

"Well," depositing some bundles in the chair in which Marjorie had been sitting, "we pretty nearly did the town, made several purchases of native workmanship—crude, but quaint—then the others wanted to go into the little theatre—it being matinée day— to see what kind of talent they produce away up here. But I didn't care for it—I was an odd one, anyway; so I took the bundles and came home."

And the look of weariness on his face plainly testified to his lack of interest in things in general.

"Well, you shouldn't have been an 'odd one,'" said his uncle, somewhat sharply, for the look was a reproof to him and nettled him, "you should have taken Marjorie along with you and given her a good time; the poor little thing has been moping herself sick all the afternoon in this lonely old inn."

Rob shot a look of surprise at him, for it was seldom that the man betrayed any irritation or ill humor before him.

"I understand that Miss Ellsworth was indisposed and did not care to go," he replied, flushing slightly.

"Is that so?" queried the elder gentleman absently. Then he added:

"She is a very sweet little body, don't you think, Rob?"

"Y—es," with a far-away look.

"That's a rather doubtful assent," said his uncle, laughing.

"Well, yes; I think Miss Ellsworth is very pretty and interesting, and she is certainly a favorite with every one, which speaks well for her amiability," Rob gravely returned; but there arose before him, as he spoke, the vision of a fair, creamy face, with earnest brown eyes, the full, intelligent brow crowned by waves of glossy brown hair, and the picture brought a look of heart-hunger into his own eyes that was pitiful to see; while he told himself that there was more depth of character mirrored in that lovely face than Marjorie Ellsworth would possess if she lived to be a hundred years old.

"Then, Rob—what do you say to trying to win her for a wife?" inquired Mr. Lancaster, thinking he might as well make a grand plunge first as last.

CHAPTER V.

LIFE FOR LIFE.

Bob lifted a look of blank amazement to his uncle at this unexpected suggestion, then flushed hotly to his temples. He was both hurt and indignant in view of it.

"Uncle Hal, don't you think you are somewhat premature, to say the least, in making such a proposition to me at this time, even if I had not been wounded beyond the possibility of ever considering it?" he inquired, in a tone that caused a responsive flush to rush to his companion's face.

"Ever!" repeated Mr. Lancaster, with some embarrassment, "that is an ominously significant word, Rob. Do you mean simply to imply that you can never marry the young lady whom I have mentioned; or that you intend to remain in a state of celibacy all your life?"

Rob's eyes were downcast, and now his countenance was very pale and gloomy as he replied:

"I told you, Uncle Hal, before we left Paris, that my life was ruined. I do not know whether I am made of different stuff from other men, but when I pledged myself to Helen Seymour, which practically I did, although there was no formal engagement to me, it meant that I gave myself—all that I was or ever hoped to be—to her for all time. It was no light, effervescing love that I bestowed upon her—that I bear her still—that I shall continue to bear her to my grave, and I shall never call any other woman wife."

Mr. Lancaster's heart sank as he listened, for the tone told him more than the words; while certain memories of his own past were aroused and awakened a despairing, responsive echo in his heart. He looked off over the mountains with troubled eyes, and a long silence fell upon the two men.

At last the elder broke it by observing gravely:

"Of course, Rob, I would not have you think I do not sympathize with, or would make light of, your trouble. I know you have suffered. I—I did not think you were quite so strongly attached to—to Miss Seymour; but when it comes to asserting that you are determined never to marry any one, it seems a —a trifle strained and melodramatic. I want you to marry. You know that you are to have all that I shall leave, when I quit this mundane sphere, which will be quite a pile; and I would like to know that it will descend to your children—perhaps a namesake among them—after you. My boy, I really would like to see you well settled in life, in the near future, with a family and interests of your own."

Rob made no reply, but his face was not encouraging, and presently his uncle resumed:

"Now—we may as well talk it out plainly while we are about it. I have become quite fond of Marjorie Ellsworth, though of course I do not mean to imply that my fondness for her is sufficient reason for your marrying her. But she is a dear, sweet girl in my opinion—pretty, well educated, and well connected. The Ellsworths were a fine family—I knew them years ago. Besides, she is tremendously fond of you——"

"Uncle Hal, surely you do not mean that she really cares for me!" exclaimed Rob, aghast.

"Yes, I do."

"What makes you think so—how do you know?"

"Well, I have eyes, and it is not difficult for one who is observing to discern the signs of the times."

Rob sprang to his feet and began to pace the piazza and evidently in great perturbation of mind.

Three times he measured the length of the platform, his uncle watching him with anxious eyes meanwhile.

At length he paused abruptly before him.

"Uncle Hal!" he burst forth excitedly, "I wish you would let me go home."

"Bless my soul, Rob, what an idea! Surely you do not mean it!" said the startled man.

"I do. I would like to go back at once. I must have something to do—some definite object in life; something to keep me from thinking, or I shall go distracted," cried Rob, with more of passion than his uncle had ever know him to manifest before.

"But, my dear boy, that would never do at all!" Mr. Lancaster returned, in a voice of dismay. "We have joined the party for the tour—our tickets are purchased for the entire route, and it would be downright shabby in us to leave them in the lurch, so abruptly, almost at the outset."

"But I have no wish to interrupt your trip, Uncle Hal; you go on with the others. Just let me have my ticket and I will take a bee-line for New York, where I will get into business with all possible despatch," Rob urged with great earnestness.

"But I could not be separated from you, Rob—we never have been yet during all the years since I took you from your mother. If you went directly home I should have to go also, and that, I think, under the circumstances, would be neither courteous nor fair toward our fellow travelers."

"But if what you have told me is true, I think it would be wrong for me to remain with the party," the young man objected, with a troubled face.

"You refer to what I said about Marjorie?"

"Yes."

"But don't you think that, with time, you could get over the sting of—of the past, at least in a measure, and make an effort to like the girl?" queried Mr. Lancaster appealingly. "I'm sure you could not find a more charming little woman for a wife if you should go the world over."

Rob was very, very white as, after a moment of fierce struggle with himself, he looked his uncle squarely in the eye and quietly observed:

"Uncle Hal, I would be glad to please you in every way possible. I feel that I owe you all honor and obedience in everything that is right and reasonable, but what I have said upon that point, I have said. I have lost the only woman I could ever love—life without her is a blank, and I shall never marry any other."

He turned abruptly as he ceased speaking, ran down the steps, and walked swiftly away from the house, while Halburton Lancaster felt that he would never retract one word of that quietly-spoken ultimatum.

The interview carried him back twenty years or more to a certain crisis in his own life, when the one woman in the world to him had been lost to him and to the agony that had followed, and which had turned his hair white as snow in a single month, and also, as it seemed, burned his heart to ashes, while over the grave of all his brightest hopes he also had sworn that no other should ever take the place of that woman.

A groan of anguish escaped him as he recalled the despair of that bygone time, and he was filled with remorse in view of his thoughtlessness and selfishness in seeking to rob his nephew of a love as tender and hopes as bright, perchance, as his own had been in those now far-off days.

"God forgive me!" he muttered, under his breath, "why did I ever do it? I never stopped to think he could suffer as I have suffered! Margaret! Margaret! if he has loved that dressmaker's daughter with a tithe of the adoration that I bestowed upon you, I have committed an unpardonable sin in being instrumental in separating him from her. But I was ambitious for him—he is all I have in the world—I thought more of his having a brilliant future than of his happiness. Oh! what spirit of evil tempted me to it, I wonder?

"Let me see," he went on, after a few moments of thought, in a tone of bitter arraignment, "let me look my sin straight in the face. I have come to the point where I can no longer shirk it. I have practically ruined four lives by what I have done. Rob's, which, of course, to me, is of more consequence than all others; Alton's, for I tempted him with my money and so dishonored him as well as myself, while that poor girl, so superior to him, will never be happy with him; and my own, for I am very sure that remorse will sting me for the remainder of my days."

As if he could no longer endure this mental agony, he now sprang to his feet and began to pace the veranda, and his face could not have been whiter if he had been dead, while there was a look in his eyes that would have melted a heart of stone.

He had been sitting near a window, half the blind to which was closed, during his conversation with Rob, and his own soliloquy. When he reached the farther end of the porch there was a slight rustling behind the blind as of some one stealing softly away. A moment later Mrs. Ellsworth emerged from the parlor of the inn into the hall and sped with fleet and nimble steps up the stairs to her room, which was di-

rectly over the one she has just left, and there was
a look of baffled rage on her face, a lurid fire in her
eyes that were not good to see.

She locked the door to keep out all intruders, then
her fury broke forth, and she took to pacing back and
forth, back and forth, muttering incoherently and
angrily to herself.

"So he will not marry my daughter! Fool! fool!"
she hissed, "and all because of his puling love for
Margaret Wilton's brat. Oh! what a complication of
circumstances! Who would have believed that a relentless fate would have involved the second genera-
tion in the same kind of a snarl that we older ones
were entangled in so many years ago! Good heavens!
I lost all in that old-time venture; am I destined to be
balked again in this? So Mr. Rob has been in love
with Helen Seymour all this time! That was what
ailed him when he broke that glass that day in Paris,
when Marjorie told him that the girl was to be
married! That was the cause of his looking so ill and
wretched when we started and made him keep so by
himself those few days of our journey. It seems that
Hal Lancaster would like him to marry Marjorie—he
is certainly fond of her; she has played her cards very
cleverly with him, and has hoodwinked him completely with those pretty, taking ways of hers. She
can do the innocent act to perfection, and I believe
she would make her fortune with it on the boards.
I am sure, though, that she is dead in love with the
boy, and it might be the making of her if she could
win him. All the same, I think there is no hope for
her there, for when Mr. Robert Eggleston delivers
himself in that quiet, but high-and-mighty way, it is
evident that he means what he says."

She stood with frowning brow and thoughtful air
looking off upon the hills for several minutes.

"Well," she went on, after awhile, "I wonder what

is to be the next move in this queer game on the checker-board of life? We really must manage some way to dip our fingers into that 'pile' of Halburton Lancaster's, for my last letter from my executor states that those Western investments look rather doubtful, and if they do not soon take a turn for the better I shall 'ere long find myself stranded. It looks as if there is but one thing left for me to do," she continued, with a resolute air and firm-set lips, "I must make a desperate effort to capture the uncle, since the nephew will not have my daughter, so, if he wants the 'dear sweet girl' for a daughter he shall have her and welcome, but he will have to take the mother with her. Bah! how white-feathered he grew over his schemes against the Seymour girl—he gave himself away pretty well, too—but it is very evident that he hasn't a suspicion whose daughter she is. Yes, it is a queer complication."

Her attention was here attracted by the return of the party from the village, and she forthwith set about making a very fetching toilet for dinner, after which she went below to join the other guests of the house, her lips wreathed with smiles and apparently in her most charming mood.

That was to be their last at Mariestad. On the morrow they were to leave for Stockholm, and after dinner had been served and the gentlemen had finished their cigars, Mrs. Ellsworth gathered all the guests of the house in the parlors and exerted herself to make the evening one long to be remembered.

They had a merry time, even Rob and Mr. Lancaster becoming so interested in the spirited entertainment that they threw off their dejection and gloom, for the time being, and joined in the various amusements of the occasion, and the affair was pronounced a grand success by every one.

The next morning our party were all en route for

Stockholm, where they spent a week, thence proceeded across the Baltic Sea, through the Gulf of Finland to St. Petersburg, at which place they made a much longer stop.

From St. Petersburg they went to Moscow, then turned southward, making Warsaw their next stopping-place, and thence into Germany, where they traveled extensively, occupying the remainder of the summer and early fall in this way.

About the first of October they again turned their face southward, and proceeded by easy stages to Constantinople.

November found them in Athens, whence they sailed across the Mediterranean Sea to Alexandria, where, after a comfortable rest, they made preparations for their travels in Egypt and the Holy Land. We cannot follow them very specifically in their wanderings, but everything had been very harmonious and enjoyable thus far along their course, while Mrs. Ellsworth had conducted herself so tactfully that she had not only become a favorite with the whole party, but had gradually established herself upon the most friendly terms with Mr. Lancaster, until it began to be whispered among their friends that there would probably be a romantic ending to their trip around the world.

Upon their return from the Nile and other points of interest in the land of the Pharaohs they stopped at Ismalia for a few days, then pushed on for Port Said, en route to the Holy Land. But just after leaving Port Said, Rob was taken suddenly and violently ill, and was obliged to stop off at a small town called El Arish, and where the party also paused for a day.

The following morning Mrs. Sturdyvant was stricken down with the same symptoms, and everybody was appalled at the situation. After a grave consultation between Mr. Lancaster and Mrs. Ellsworth, it was decided best for the party to go on, taking Marjorie with them, continue their sight-seeing as laid down in their itinerary, while, as soon as the condition of the invalids would permit, those left behind would rejoin them at some point to be decided upon later on.

Marjorie openly rebelled against this arrangement, as far as she was concerned; for she was almost wild in view of Rob's critical state, and she insisted that she must remain to assist in caring for him, as well as for her aunt.

But her mother was peremptory, and every one else claimed that it would be unwise for her to do as she wished, and she was forced to yield, although she did so under protest and with a very sore heart.

And then for those remaining behind there followed a fierce battle for life such as very few are called upon to fight during their mortal existence.

No efficient nurses could be procured in the town, and the physician, who was called, was not one to inspire one with over-much confidence; consequently most of the responsibility during this trying time rested upon Mr. Lancaster and Mrs. Ellsworth.

Mrs. Sturdyvant was not dangerously ill, but was so debilitated, so weak and miserable, that she was unable to lift her head from her pillow during the first week, and when she finally did get up, could only lie idly in a hammock in the shade and submit to be waited upon by a native woman who had been secured for that purpose.

With Rob, however, the case was far different. He was a terribly sick boy, and required constant attention day and night.

For three long weeks he did not know one lucid interval, and, although not violent in his delirium, muttered continually of "Helen" and a thousand things associated with their school life and their love for each other, which plainly betrayed where his heart had been during the long months of his roving, and drove Mr. Lancaster almost frantic with grief and remorse.

Being wholly unused to such wearing anxiety and close confinement, the man often gave out, and then Mrs. Ellsworth was the only one left to fill the breach.

These trying experiences brought out powers which not even she herself had dreamed that she possessed.

From the outset she had discarded all finery, but arraying herself in pure white linen, with her pretty hair tucked up under a becoming cap, yet looking more charming than when in full dress, she seemed for the first time in her life—as she constituted herself nurse and maid in general—a truly womanly woman, and her sister-in-law regarded her in amazement.

At last there came a time when every one went about the house with bated breath, treading noiselessly with bare or softly shod feet, while those who watched beside Rob's couch scarce moved or spoke for many, many hours.

Mr. Lancaster had lost all hope, and plainly betrayed the despair that had taken possession of him. He was practically of no use in the sick-room during this crisis, although he had hitherto been most helpful.

As hope waned his strength seemed to go with it, until Mrs. Ellsworth began to fear that she would soon have another patient upon her hands.

It would be impossible to portray the man's mental suffering as he sat beside his dear boy's couch and reviewed the last two years of his life. If agony could expiate his temptation and sin it would seem that his atonement must have been complete.

Mrs. Ellsworth, however, seemed to rise to the occasion with the increased demands upon her.

For two days and as many nights when the crisis

came she never left her post by Rob's bed, except to snatch sufficient food to sustain her strength.

All medicines had been abandoned, for they had lost all influence upon the patient, who lay absolutely unconscious, breathing weakly and without moving hand or foot.

From a bowl of nourishment that stood beside her— some strong, appetizing broth which she had made with her own hands according to her sister's directions —Mrs. Ellsworth fed the apparently dying young man a spoonful every few moments, and even though she could not see that he swallowed it, she did not relax her efforts to sustain his strength.

"I will save him if it lies in the power of mortal to do so," she said to herself over and over, her white teeth locked together with an indomitable purpose, "and then Halburton Lancaster shall give me—a life for a life."

CHAPTER VI.

"ASK WHAT YOU WILL!"

MIDNIGHT of that last terrible day drew near, and there was not a sound in that sick-room nor within the house. In a corner there burned a dim oriental lamp, that shed a dull, red glow throughout the apartment, every window of which was open to admit a cool breeze that was blowing inland from the sea.

Mr. Lancaster, utterly worn out with grief and hopeless watching, had fallen asleep in a hammock that had been swung across another corner of the room.

Mrs. Ellsworth, pale and hollow-eyed, and almost at the end of her own strength and fortitude, was still watching Rob's every faintly drawn breath, and faithfully feeding him from time to time. She had her watch on a small table beside her, and she glanced fearfully at it every now and then, as the long hand moved slowly toward the hour of twelve.

When it lacked five minutes of it she held her own breath while she counted the seconds, and felt as if the supreme moment was very near.

The day had been intensely hot, but when the wind had changed, sweeping in freshly from the ocean, Rob had been covered with soft, warm blankets to protect him from the chill in the air. The five minutes passed; the hour-hand swept on upon its ceaseless round, but as yet there was no visible change in the patient. Mrs. Ellsworth slipped her hand underneath the bedclothes and took one of Rob's gently within her clasp.

It was cold, and a shiver of dread ran over her.

Then all at once her whole soul arose in rebellion against the thought of death.

"He shall not die! He cannot die," she whispered to herself, with rigid lips.

She continued to hold his hand in hers, and then, without realizing that she was even drowsy, her head fell back against the rocker in which she was sitting, and tired nature asserted itself—she also slept.

What awakened her she never knew, but all at once every sense and nerve in her body was on the alert, and her heart bounded into her throat as she suddenly became conscious that the hand she was holding had grown warm and its palm was covered with a gentle perspiration!

Had it been caused by the renewing of vitality, or had the clasp of her own hand produced the warmth and moisture?

She glanced at the figure on the bed.

His chest arose and fell regularly, though feebly, and he seemed to be sleeping naturally; he was no longer in a state of stupor. Her eyes sought her watch.

It was half-past twelve, and she knew that she had lost herself for nearly thirty minutes, and that while she slept the crisis had passed.

Rob was surely better, though, even now, his life hung by a very slender thread; but, with a sense of triumph such as she had rarely known, she vowed that he should live.

There was a spirit-lamp on the table beside her, also a small tin cup, and she noiselessly proceeded to heat some of the broth against the time her patient should awake.

She did not have long to wait. A little after one o'clock Rob's white lids unclosed for the first time in forty-eight hours, and though he was too weak to turn his head upon the pillow, his glance met hers with a look of recognition.

The woman was exultant, though she did not betray it by word or sign.

She simply held a spoon to his lips, and he voluntarily sipped its contents, then glanced at the cup in her other hand to signify that he wanted more.

She fed him all that he had strength to take, whereupon he immediately dropped asleep again.

She then laid another blanket over him, after which she wrapped a fleecy shawl about herself and sank back in her chair with a soft sigh of relief, and feeling that it would be safe to relax her vigilance for awhile and snatch some much needed rest. Three times after that she gave him nourishment, which he seemed to eagerly crave; then, as he sank into a sounder, more natural slumber just as day was beginning to dawn, Mrs. Ellsworth gently awakened Mr. Lancaster and drew him out of the room, for she would not speak a word there to disturb Rob.

"What is it?" the man tremblingly inquired. "Oh! why have you allowed me to sleep the whole night through? Is—is he gone?"

"Hush!" she said, laying her hand upon his arm, "you must be calm. Rob is better; he has aroused several times since midnight, and taken considerable nourishment."

"Better! Oh, are you sure?" Mr. Lancaster gasped, with something like a sob.

"Yes, I am sure; and he will get well if we continue to give him the right care," Mrs. Ellsworth replied, and then told him how and when the change for the better had occurred.

Mr. Lancaster clasped the hand that still rested upon his arm and raised it to his lips.

"God bless you! You have saved him," he said gratefully. "But you should have awakened me and allowed me to share your vigil. I have been very selfish and inconsiderate."

She smiled almost fondly into his face.

"You needed the rest; a man can never endure watching like a woman," she said. "I did not arouse you because it was not necessary, and, besides, it would have disturbed Rob to have had any movement in the room—he is too weak to bear any confusion. But now, if you are refreshed, I will leave you with him and go for a nap."

"Indeed, you must, you dear woman! You are worn out; you are white as a ghost from your ceaseless watching of the last forty-eight hours," returned her companion, with a pitiful glance at her wan face, yet thinking that he had never seen her so lovely.

And at that moment, in the subdued light of the early dawn, in her spotless dress and pretty lace cap, and with that grave, earnest look on her face, she seemed to him, in the first flush of his gratitude, almost like a saint, for she had saved his boy.

She gave him directions regarding feeding Rob if he wakened again, but cautioned him not to talk—not even to speak a word to him.

"Let him rest," she said, "he must make no effort, even to think, until he is stronger."

Then, nodding a smiling adieu to him, she glided away and sought her own room, where she sank, weary and exhausted, upon her bed.

She slept heavily for two hours, and then, unable to cast off her responsibility, stole back to the sick-room.

Rob was resting quietly and had not aroused once during her absence.

She made Mr. Lancaster go down-stairs for some breakfast while she watched by the patient.

When he returned she prepared some fresh nourishment for the sick one, and then went to help Mrs.

Sturdyvant dress and tell her the good news, while they ate their morning meal together. The report was like a bracing tonic to the weak woman, who had suffered keenly in her mind during the trials of the last few weeks, and because of her inability to share the heavy responsibilities of her companions.

After breakfast Mrs. Ellsworth went back to bed and slept restfully until noon.

When she returned to the sick-room again Rob was awake and smiled a feeble welcome at her, then took with evident relish the glass of warm milk which she had brought him.

From that time he improved rapidly, for he grew hungry as a young bear with returning strength, and at the end of a week was able to be bolstered up in bed.

Still another seven days and he was up, walking feebly about the house, while it was thought that by the end of one more week it would be safe for him to resume his journey, when they would all go straight through to Calcutta, by easy stages, and rejoin their party, who would arrive there early in March and remain for a couple of weeks, or rather, they would make their headquarters there while they visited other points of interest in the vicinity of that "City of Palaces."

The good news of Rob's rapid convalescence, as well as of Mrs. Sturdyvant's full recovery, had already been telegraphed to them, and when word was received regarding when and where they would all meet again, everybody became elated and happy once more.

During all this time Mrs. Ellsworth had continued to carry herself in the most delightful and exemplary manner. She petted Rob during the tedious weeks of his recovery in the most motherly way imaginable; she prepared him the most appetizing and dainty dishes; read to him hour after hour, told him charming stories and incidents, and was a perfect sunbeam in the house—a veritable oasis in the desert of that weary waiting.

Mr. Lancaster declared that there was no one like her for patience, inventive genius, and sweetness of disposition. He firmly believed that Rob would have died but for her tender care and devotion, her tireless watching, and, consequently, his gratitude knew no bounds; while, besides all this, she had added many dainty touches to the comparatively rude house they were in—though it was one of the best in the place—thus contributing much to the comfort and enjoyment of the other members of the family.

To Mrs. Sturdyvant the woman was a marvel, for she had been a perfect butterfly all her life, floating hither and thither, wherever she could find sunshine and pleasure, and she had not believed her capable of rising to such heights of self-abnegation as she had manifested during those trying weeks at El Arish. She felt sure that there must be some selfish motive behind it all, and she thought she knew what that motive was; and yet, in spite of that, she was amazed in view of her powers of endurance, both mental and physical, and at the invariable cheerfulness and sweetness which she manifested.

"I would not detract one iota from the merit of all that she has done," she said to herself, while thinking these things over, "for, whatever purpose has actuated her, there is no question that she has achieved wonders—she has wrought a good work in saving Rob, and she has been very good to me, as well. All the same, she has a long head, and I believe she is playing a clever and desperate game to win Hal Lancaster. I wonder if——"

But what she wondered was cut short by the entrance of Mrs. Ellsworth herself, and so remained a secret in her own breast.

The journey, when they were once more en route, instead of taxing Rob's strength, as his uncle had feared, seemed to do him good; he continued to improve every day, and, by the time they rejoined their party in Calcutta, excepting the fact that he was still rather thin, and looked a trifle delicate, he appeared almost like himself again. He said, indeed, that he "felt like a new creature, as if he had been entirely made over."

There was general rejoicing upon the evening of their reunion, in honor of which great preparations had been made. The party had taken rooms in one of the finest hotels of the city, and a grand dinner was served them in a private dining-room, where toasts and speeches were made, and champagne drank in glad commemoration of Rob's recovered health, and their joy over being all together again.

Marjorie bloomed out into brighter beauty than usual. She had had a new and very fetching costume made for the occasion, and seemed supremely happy and light-hearted.

Rob, however, was careful not to encourage any tender sentiments in connection with himself. He greeted her cordially, as he did every one else in the party, and when, after dinner, they all repaired to the ballroom, where a brilliant hop was being given for the benefit of the guests of the house, he divided his attentions equally among the various young ladies whom he knew.

During these festivities, Mrs. Ellsworth stole out upon a balcony from one of the long windows of the dance-hall, and which commanded a fine view of the brilliantly lighted city. She was anxious and harassed, for she had found letters awaiting her from her executor, who informed her that the investments, to which reference had previously been made in other letters, had all collapsed, and she would never be able to realize five per cent. of their face value.

This was a severe blow to her, although, excepting Mrs. Sturdyvant, she kept the matter to herself, for reasons of her own, for it would so deplete her income that she would be obliged to exercise the strictest economy in order to exist, unless her sister-in-law would give her and Marjorie a home, or she could achieve the matrimonial project for which she had been scheming.

Time was flying, and she seemed no nearer the goal of her fond aspirations than when she had left Mariestad, where she had formed the resolution to win Halburton Lancaster.

The man had been as kind as could be to her, anticipating every need and wish, and showing her every possible attention; but he had shown not the slightest disposition to yield himself a slave to her charms in the way she most desired, and she was very anxious to have her future settled before the party sailed for the United States.

She was becoming weary of travel, for the first time in her life. The five or six weeks at El Arish had been a tremendous strain upon her, for, in spite of her "sweetness," she had hated her duties, and it was only by the exercise of all her will-power, backed by the determination to win Mr. Lancaster, that she had been able to undergo that trying ordeal.

Now she was determined to bring matters to a crisis, if possible. If she was successful, she felt that she could go on with the party with a good grace, and fling care and worry to the winds; if she failed, she would leave them immediately, and go directly back to America, for she still had a little money, which she would risk in one desperate venture to retrieve her fallen fortunes.

She was thinking of these things now, as she sat

upon the balcony—in fact, she had come out to be by herself, and reflect upon them.

She could not have been there more than fifteen or twenty minutes, however, when Marjorie and Mr. Lancaster came and stood in the window behind her, although they could not see her, for she was sitting in the shadow of a pillar that supported the roof of the balcony.

The girl had immediately resumed her friendly relations with the man upon his arrival, and was now telling him something about the trip during their separation.

"Of course, it has all been very nice and interesting," she observed; "and Mr. and Mrs. Welling have been almost like a father and mother to me; but I could not help feeling very anxious about mamma, and R—and the rest of you, you know."

"That was but natural, my child," returned Mr. Lancaster, but with a twinge as she cut Rob's name short. "I know it must have been very trying to have been separated from your friends for so long, and to know that they were in that fever-stricken country. But, I am sure, I do not know what we should have done without your mother; she has been a perfect wonder to us all! I cannot understand how she managed to keep up her own strength, for she is not a rugged-looking woman, and she did not spare herself. I know next to nothing about sickness, and I felt as helpless as a child all through Rob's fearful illness, except when she took the helm, and gave her orders."

"Mamma seems well, though I think she does look a little thin and worn," responded Marjorie reflectively. "I am surprised, too, at what you have told me, for I did not imagine that she would be equal to anything of the kind."

"Ha! ha! Marjorie, my dear, you perceive you have

not appreciated your mother's abilities," Mrs. Ellsworth here laughingly interposed, for she did not care to sit there and listen to their discussion of her.

She leaned forward into the light, as she spoke, and made a lovely picture of herself, for the colored lanterns hanging above her cast a rose-hued glow upon her that was very effective.

She was beautifully dressed, in rich white satin, with an exquisite black lace over-dress, and, Mr. Lancaster having sent her a box of beautiful flowers before dinner, she had pinned some bright red roses upon her corsage, and they made a vivid spot of color against the dead black and white of her costume.

"Why, mamma! Are you out there?" exclaimed Marjorie in surprise, while she bent forward to get a better view of her.

"Yes; I felt a little tired and heated, and thought I would like to get away from the confusion and glare of the crowded room. Will you come out? The night is lovely."

"No, I believe not," Marjorie returned, "for I have promised Will Welling the next waltz, and he will be looking for me."

The three chatted together for a few minutes, then, the young man coming to her, Marjorie left her companions, and went upon the floor.

"If you will not regard me as an intruder, I shall be glad to join you out there, Mrs. Ellsworth," Mr. Lancaster observed as the girl disappeared.

The woman's heart bounded like a thing of life at his words.

"No, indeed; I shall be glad of company," she cordially replied, "for," with a soft sigh, "I believe I was getting a trifle low-spirited out here alone with my thoughts."

Mr. Lancaster stepped out upon the balcony, drew a chair to her side, and sat down.

"I hope you are not feeling ill," he remarked, with a note of concern in his tones that thrilled her again.

"Oh, no; I am perfectly well, but—I found some letters here, from my man of business, that are rather depressing. There have been some losses, which—which make the future look somewhat doubtful for me," she explained, hoping to work upon his sympathies, and lead him on.

"Ah! I am sorry to hear that," he remarked, with kindly interest. "Perhaps, when we get back to New York, you will allow me to investigate matters for you, and see if I cannot straighten them out."

"You are very kind," Mrs. Ellsworth murmured in a low tone.

"Why should I not be? What do I not owe you?" said Mr. Lancaster, with a quiver of earnest gratitude in his voice. "Why, my friend, you have but to ask what you will of me, and it shall be granted you, 'even'—as in the words of one of old—'to the half of my kingdom.'"

CHAPTER VII.

PERFECT COMPREHENSION.

Mrs. Ellsworth began to tremble with excitement, in view of what her companion had said.

"Could it be possible that the hour for her triumph had come at last?" she asked herself.

At all events, she realized that the man was in a tender mood, and she resolved to make the most of her opportunity.

"That is a sweeping statement," she retorted, with a light laugh, while she toyed with the roses upon her breast—an act which attracted her companion's attention to the fact that she was wearing upon her heart a portion of his floral offering. "How do you know but what I may ask for somebody's head, as was done in that olden time to which you refer?"

"Ah, but I have no Herodias to deal with," he retorted in the same vein. Then he added in a grave, moved tone: "But, jesting aside, I can never forget those weary weeks at El Arish! When I look back, and recall what you did for my poor boy, I feel that, as far as I personally am concerned, the world laid at your feet would not be an adequate return for his precious life."

"How he loves that fellow!" said Marien Ellsworth to herself. But, aloud, she very modestly remarked:

"You make too much of my services, which, I assure you, were most willingly given, for I, too, had become very fond of Rob, and—why!" with a sudden burst of feeling, "of course, I could not see him lying there, with the fever burning his dear life away, without making a desperate effort to save him!"

"I know; you forgot yourself entirely—especially during those last forty-eight hours, when all hope had deserted me. Oh, I can never forget it—never! So you are to regard me as your stanch friend for all time—you are to call upon me in any emergency, and you will find me ever ready to respond, to any possible extent."

"Even to the half of your kingdom?" repeated his companion archly.

"Yes; and that would be far too small a return."

"Do not be too sure, for I may take you at your word," said the wily widow, leaning toward him, and lifting a smiling but tender glance to him.

"Try me, and see. Truly, my dear Mrs. Ellsworth, I never was more in earnest in my life. What can I do for you, to prove to you how grateful I am?" and, in his earnestness, he laid his hand lightly upon the slender, jeweled one that rested upon the arm of her chair.

She laughed out musically again.

"I suppose you cannot lay claim to a very extensive 'kingdom' if you count the people in it," she said. "It's practically composed of two individuals, and Rob doubtless counts for half, in your estimation."

"Yes, fully that; but, of course, I can't give you Rob—he is at his own disposal," was the laughing rejoinder, while the man had not thought of himself, nor a suspicion of the precipice he was approaching.

"Well, then—suppose—suppose I claim the—other half?"

The woman breathed with downcast eyes and heaving bosom.

Mr. Lancaster sat suddenly erect, and drew a long breath of astonishment.

But, even then, he did not believe she was in

earnest; he honestly thought she was merely carrying her jesting mood and smile a little farther, just for the sake of being facetious.

But, for all that, he was amazed—shocked at the audacious construction which she had dared to put upon his words, even though it were but in jest.

He found himself in an extremely awkward position, and, for a moment, he was at a loss to know how to reply to her.

Then he was impelled to take it for granted that she was only making light of the subject, and answer her in the same strain.

"Really, my friend, you'll have to name something of more value," he retorted, laughing again. "That would be the poorest possible return for what you have done. Rob's young life is not to be named in the same breath. We old codgers, who have grown hoary crowned"—running his fingers nervously through his snow-white hair—"and passé are possibly of very little account in the world."

Mrs. Ellsworth flushed crimson, with mingled anger and mortification, to have him evade her thus; but, having risked everything upon this desperate leap, she was determined that she could not beat a cowardly retreat.

"You undervalue yourself, Mr. Lancaster, and the 'hoary crown,' as you term it, is, to me, a veritable crown of glory," she gravely returned, and with an air which plainly indicated that she was in no light frame of mind, if he was.

He leaned forward, and searched her face.

"Surely, Mrs. Ellsworth, you cannot have been in earnest in what you have said!" he remarked, in a tone of grave surprise.

"Why not?" she questioned, meeting his glance for an instant, then averting her eyes, and flushing again.

"But—you forget——"

"What?"

"My past!"

"No; I have forgotten nothing."

"And did you really think that such an arrangement could be possible?" the man inquired in a wondering tone.

"Why not, I ask you?" she demanded, with a touch of bravado, but shrinking, as if she had been struck.

"You ought to know that it would not be possible, Marien," he returned in a tone there was no mistaking, and addressing her by her given name, for the first time in many years; "for," and he bent nearer to her, and whispered something in her ear.

"Ah! Is that so? Then you love her still!" she exclaimed, with white lips, and in a harsh, rasping voice.

"Yes; there has not been a day, an hour, or a moment that I have not yearned for her with all my soul!" said Halburton Lancaster, with a wail of despair in his tone that betrayed he was laboring under intense and painful emotion.

Marien Ellsworth now sat erect, and threw back her proud head defiantly.

She was deeply humiliated by the failure of her scheme—for she knew it had failed miserably—while, at the same time, she was enraged anew against her old-time rival, who had so successfully supplanted her in the hearts of two men.

"I cannot understand such unexplained fidelity," she sneered. "I cannot understand why you have lived alone all these years, if you have yearned for her like that—why you have not sought her, and tried your fate again."

The man beside her groaned at the heartless taunt.

"I have sought her everywhere," he said; "for, as soon as I recovered my senses after that terrible scene, I realized that I had done her a fearful wrong, and I would have pleaded on my knees for her forgiveness."

"Then, you have never seen her—never heard anything of her—since that day?" interposed Mrs. Ellsworth, with a suppressed eagerness which, had he not been so absorbed in his own sad thoughts, would have impressed him as somewhat strange.

"No; I could never obtain the slightest clue to her whereabouts; she seemed to have disappeared out of the world as completely as a meteor when it falls into space. I feared that she might be in need of money, after she so rashly fled from her home; and, even though she never could have forgiven me, or accepted anything from me, yet I would have found some way to provide for her, and to throw protection about her. She may be somewhere in the world to-day—she may be old, and faded from toiling for her living; she may be dead—I know not; but, living or dead, I love her as wholly, as devotedly, as madly as in the days of our youth. And so, you understand——"

"Oh, yes; I could not fail to understand," suddenly interposed Mrs. Ellsworth in a sharp, shrill tone, as she rose, and stood, straight and tall, before him. "But allow me to say that Margaret and John Wilton and you were a trio of fools, whose equal I have never met—unless, perhaps, I except myself, because of my recent folly."

"Pray, Mrs. Ellsworth, let me say——" Mr. Lancaster began.

But she swept past him with the air of an offended queen, and re-entered the hotel, going straight to her own room, and was seen among the guests no more that night.

Mr. Lancaster sat for a long time where she had left him, and, from his bowed head and dejected attitude, it was evident that his reflections were far from being of a cheerful nature.

An hour later, Mrs. Ellsworth sought Mrs. Sturdyvant, and her pale, haggard face plainly testified that she had been having a terrible battle with herself since her interview with Mr. Lancaster.

"Eliza, I am going to cut the party, and go directly home," she abruptly announced, as she threw herself wearily into a chair.

"What on earth do you mean, Marien?" demanded her sister-in-law in undisguised amazement.

"Just what I say, Eliza. I am going to start for home to-morrow night. You know what disastrous news I have had from Jennings, and I can't rest until I know just how I stand with the world."

"Nonsense, Marien!" retorted Mrs. Sturdyvant, but studying her companion's face curiously. "Your tickets are paid for, and you might as well have the full benefit of them, and see the country as you go; while it is certainly the opportunity of a lifetime for Marjorie."

"Well, you know very well that tickets are not all that is necessary; it takes money, and plenty of it, too, as we are living, to foot the hotel bills; and I am sure, I don't know where I am to get it."

Mrs. Sturdyvant looked thoughtful for a few moments.

"I suppose I might lend you enough for that," she said at length.

"If I borrow, I do not know that I can ever pay," sharply returned the unhappy woman. "No," she added in a tone of decision; "I shall leave for Hongkong, where we take the steamer to-morrow evening, taking Marjorie with me. There will, doubtless, be other English and American tourists returning to the United States, so we shall not feel that we are traveling alone."

"You might leave Marjorie with me," said Mrs. Sturdyvant reflectively. "I do not like to have her lose all our delightful trips through China and Japan."

"I shall do no such thing! Do you think I am going all that journey by myself?" was the irritable response.

"I was only thinking of Marjorie's advantage in having the travel with me," said her sister-in-law kindly, "and other benefits which might arise, if she remained with the party. How is she getting on with Mr. Eggleston?"

"Oh, I gave that up long ago!" with a weary sigh.

"How about your other scheme?"

At this question, without the slightest warning, and to Mrs. Sturdyvant's astonishment, Mrs. Ellsworth burst into passionate sobbing.

She rarely cried, no matter how harassing or perplexing the circumstances, and Mrs. Sturdyvant knew at once that something more trying than usual must have occurred to upset her like this.

"Don't, Marien!" she said regretfully. "I would not have referred to the matter; but, of course, I have not been blind during the last three months, and could understand a thing or two, even if you had not hinted at your intentions before we left Paris, and, naturally, I felt interested to know how you were coming on with your plans."

"That is all off, too," sobbed the disheartened woman, who felt utterly humiliated by the abject failure of the bold step she had ventured upon that night. "I may as well make a clean breast of everything, and own up that that is one reason why I am determined to go home," she went on, after a moment. "I have just had an interview with Mr. Lancaster, during which I—I sounded him on that old affair, and, hoping that would bring him to the point; but he frankly confessed that he loves Margaret Wil-

ton to-day as madly as he ever did; to use his own
words, he 'yearns for her every day, and hour, and
moment of his life,' and, having lived all these years
cherishing her image in his heart, he has no desire
to ever change his condition, and no intention of ever
doing so."

"Yes, I was sure that he would feel like that," said
Mrs. Sturdyvant quietly. "He was never a vacillat-
ing man, and I have always felt that he was made
of too loyal stuff ever to waver in his allegiance to
the woman he loved."

"Well, I think that both he and John Wilton made
a couple of idiots of themselves to break their hearts
and ruin their lives over a girl who did not care a
straw for them!" passionately exclaimed Mrs. Ellsworth, as she wiped away the tears that were already
beginning to dry on her hot cheeks.

"Oh, but, Marien, I am sure that Margaret adored
her husband; she proved that to me when I saw her
a year and a half ago," gravely returned Mrs. Sturdyvant. "I own that she was rash in leaving him and
her beautiful home as she did, and I believe that, if she
had waited until all parties had grown calmer and
more reasonable, she would to-day have been one of
the happiest women in the world."

A long, fierce hiss here parted Marien Ellsworth's
lips.

"How I hate her!" she added viciously; "and if ever
our paths in life cross again, I'll make her feel it a
hundredfold! And, to think, after all that has gone
before, that it is her daughter who has stood in the
way of Marjorie's prospects!" she concluded, with
flaming eyes and crimson cheeks.

"What do you mean, Marien?" cried her companion
in startled surprise.

"Well," said the woman, with an embarrassed but
bitter laugh, "I never meant that anybody should

know the truth, and I let it out without thinking just now; but you may as well have the whole story, since I have aroused your curiosity," whereupon she related the conversation which she had overheard pass between Rob and Mr. Lancaster, on the porch of the inn, the night before the party left Mariestad in Sweden.

"Really, this is a very complex state of affairs; and now I understand a good many things that have hitherto puzzled me," Mrs. Sturdyvant exclaimed. "For instance, Rob's agitation, that day in Paris, when Marjorie told of Helen Seymour's marriage to that Alton fellow, and his ill turn and depression afterward. It certainly is very strange that your daughter and Margaret's should run up against each other in their love affairs in much the same way that you two did. Does Marjorie know?"

"I am not sure—I have never exchanged a word with her about it; but she is very shrewd, and it would not surprise me if she had managed to fathom something of the affair during her acquaintance with the girl," replied Marjorie's mother.

"Well, it is very queer! But I suppose Mr. Lancaster does not know who Helen Seymour is—that she is the daughter of the woman whom he has loved all his life," musingly observed Mrs. Sturdyvant.

No; and he never shall, if I can help it!" muttered her companion between her teeth.

"How vindictive and selfish you are, Marien," was the reproving response to this outburst.

"Indeed! I suppose my own disappointments, past and present, count for nothing?" snapped the angry woman irritably.

"I believe you are only reaping what you have sown," said her companion gravely.

"Ugh! Don't begin to preach, Eliza!" with an impatient shrug.

"I wonder," thoughtfully remarked Mrs. Sturdyvant, after a pause of several moments, "how it would do for me to give Hal Lancaster a hint of who Helen Seymour is, and——"

"Eliza Sturdyvant, if you do, I shall hate you, too, till my dying day!" passionately interposed her listener. "Oh, I was a fool to tell you what I have! I never meant you should know; but I am well-nigh distracted to-night, and it escaped me before I was aware of it. Besides, you said you promised Margaret that you would keep her secret."

"I know I did; and, since the girl is married, there would be no use in stirring up matters; if she was still single, I believe, for Mr. Eggleston's sake, I would risk it. No; I think I will keep my promise. I will not meddle in what does not concern me," Mrs. Sturdyvant thoughtfully responded.

Mrs. Ellsworth arose, with a sigh of relief, for not for the world would she have had Mr. Lancaster learn the truth regarding the woman she so hated; there should never be a reconciliation between them, if she could prevent it, even though she knew she would reap no personal benefit by keeping them apart.

"Well,", she observed at length, and rising, "I have told you my plans, Eliza—I am going home at once; I suppose, though, from what you have said, that you will not feel like coming with us?"

"No, I think not, Marien," the lady replied. "I probably shall never have another opportunity to take this trip, and feel as if I would like to avail myself of all the privileges to which I am entitled. I wish you would be sensible, and keep on with us. What if your matrimonial plans have failed? Rob and Mr. Lancaster are both true gentlemen, and they will do nothing to make you uncomfortable. I am sure, it will seem very strange to the other members of the party to have you leave us so suddenly, and start off alone on such a long journey by yourselves."

"I can't help it!" retorted Mrs. Ellsworth, growing hot and cold by turns, as she thought of what she had done that night, and knew that she could never face Halburton Lancaster again with any degree of composure. "I shall simply state that business complications require me to hasten home—which is the truth, though it makes me almost heart-sick to think of what awaits me there, if things are really as bad as Mr. Jennings has written."

"You'd better let me lend you enough to tide over the present," urged her sister-in-law kindly.

"No; I shall go," was the dogged reply; and, with that ultimatum, she went back to her own room, where she passed a restless, miserable night.

She announced her plans the next morning, and everybody was profuse in their regrets, in view of her decision, and begged her to reconsider it, for she really had been a most enjoyable campagnon de voyage.

She would not retract, however, and she and Marjorie spent the day in packing and making ready for their hurried flitting.

But Marjorie was very unreconciled to this un-looked-for move, for she had not yet relinquished all hope of winning Rob, in spite of the unmistakable reserve which he had manifested toward her upon rejoining the party. She pleaded and begged that her mother would allow her to remain with her aunt during the remainder of the trip, but the woman was inexorable.

Mr. Lancaster was greatly relieved upon learning of her intentions. Indeed, he had almost been tempted to do the same thing, for he realized that all future relations between himself and Mrs. Ellsworth could not fail to be strained and uncomfortable, and would mar all his pleasure during the remainder of the trip.

He was very kind to her, however, greeted her as if nothing unusual had occurred, and exerted himself to provide every possible comfort for her contemplated journey, even to telegraphing ahead, to ascertain if there were other American tourists whom she could join when the steamer sailed from Hongkong.

The reply stated that there would be a large company, and everybody felt much easier in view of their departure.

The entire party went to the station to see the travelers off, and they were laden, not only with good wishes, but with flowers, dainties of all kinds to eat, and plenty of entertaining books, to help them pass the time enjoyably.

CHAPTER VIII.

A WOMAN IN GRAY.

MARIEN ELLSWORTH was an entirely different woman after leaving her party and was started on her homeward journey. All her sweetness, affability, and smiles had fled.

Two deep wrinkles settled between her brows, and an expression of irritability and discontent overshadowed her whole face. She was fretful and impatient with Marjorie, and became so generally disagreeable that the girl finally let her entirely alone, and tried to interest herself in the books, papers, and various mysterious boxes which Mr. Lancaster had piled upon the seat beside her when he took leave of her.

The ride to Hongkong was somewhat tedious and uninteresting, as the weather was unpleasant, and there were no people on board the train with whom our two travelers could make friends, and it was with a feeling of great relief that they finally found themselves on board one of the great Pacific Mail liners —the "China"—and in the midst of English-speaking people, a goodly number of whom were their own countrymen.

But the voyage proved to be tempestuous, and both Marjorie and her mother were ill during the greater portion of it after leaving Yokohama, and were truly thankful when it was ended, and they finally set foot on terra firma once more at San Francisco.

They stopped in this city only long enough to recruit a little, and then took passage over the Union

Pacific Railway direct for New York. While passing through Colorado, they were very much impressed with the magnificant scenery, and, as they drew near to the far-famed city of Colorado Springs, Mrs. Ellsworth suddenly informed Marjorie that she had decided to stop off there for a few days.

"Why, mamma! I thought you were in a great hurry to get to New York?" the girl observed in surprise.

"Well, and so I am; but I have heard so much about the place—of Manitou and Pike's Peak—that I am impelled to have a look at them. Besides, I am so weary of this car, and our close quarters, I absolutely must get some rest in a decent bed for a few nights."

So the conductor was interviewed, and the stop arranged for. As they were alighting from the train at the Colorado Springs station, Mrs. Ellsworth's glance fell upon a portly man, who was conversing with another gentleman upon the platform. She gave a gasp of astonishment, while, he, at the same moment, caught sight of her, and started forward, with extended hand, to greet her.

"Mr. Jennings! Of all the people in the world, how does it happen that I run across you here?" panted the excited woman.

"Well, I have been in this city for about two weeks, on business connected with some mines in which I have an interest," the gentleman explained. "But," he added, "I am no less astonished to meet you here. I imagined you were, just about now, in the land of chrysanthemums, lotus-blossoms, and jinrikishas."

"I should have been, but I got short of money, and so anxious over your last letters that I could not enjoy myself another moment, so left the party, and started for home, to find out the worst," Mrs. Ellsworth explained, the anxious harassed look returning to her face.

Mr. Jennings also looked grave at this reference to her financial difficulties.

"Are you going to stop here long?" he inquired.

"No; only a few days. It was merely a whim of mine, our getting off here, for at first I intended to push straight through to New York. But I was tired—almost car-sick, in fact—and wanted to see this place, Manitou and the canyons. I am inclined to think, though, that fate ordained the stop, so that I should meet you," Mrs. Ellsworth observed, with a faint smile.

"Well, it does seem a peculiar coincidence," the gentleman remarked. Then he inquired: "Have you settled upon any place to go?"

"No; I am utterly at sea here; can't you direct us to some good hotel that is not too expensive?"

"I am stopping at the Alta Vista—the prices are not so high as at The Antlers, and I am sure you would be comfortable there," Mr. Jennings returned.

Mrs. Ellsworth assented to this proposition, whereupon a carriage was called, and the party proceeded to the hotel, where the weary travelers found pleasant rooms, and where they gave themselves up to rest and refreshing themselves for the remainder of the morning.

After lunch, Mr. Jennings sought them again, saying he was at their disposal, if they would signify what they wanted to do, or where they wished to go.

But Mrs. Ellsworth declared that she must first have a square business talk with him, for she wanted to know exactly how she stood with the world.

Again the man's face fell. It was evident that what he had to tell her was not of an encouraging nature.

"Well," he began, with manifest embarrassment, "I

am obliged to confess that what I wrote you about those Western investments was only to prepare you for the worst upon your return. They have not only collapsed, but assessments have been levied upon your —— Railroad stocks, so the outlook seems to portend either sending good money after bad, or letting your shares go by the board."

"Heavens and earth! Do you mean to tell me that I have absolutely no resources left?" demanded Mrs. Ellsworth, and growing pale and faint from apprehension.

"It looks awfully like it—unless you've got something back of all, that I know nothing about," replied her attorney reluctantly.

"I haven't—not a dollar!" groaned the miserable woman. "But tell me about it," she commanded almost fiercely; "I must know the whole story."

And the gentleman proceeded to go into details, explaining the how and why, the result of which was to prove that the heretofore giddy butterfly of the world and fashion was, or very soon would be, literally penniless.

"You still have those shares in the co-operative business in Chicago," he observed in a would-be cheerful tone, and trying hard not to see the white, pinched face and despairing eyes opposite him. "They paid about two per cent. last year—I don't know as you will get as much this year, for that business is pretty near flat just now; but maybe you can dispose of them, if you need a little ready money."

"Oh, you know, that would be but a drop in the bucket! Heavens! what—am—I—going—to—do?" cried the woman in a hopeless tone.

"That seems to be a problem, I confess," her companion remarked, as he hitched uneasily in his chair. "I am awfully sorry things have turned out so," he added regretfully, "but, of course, I could control neither the Western investments nor the railroad stock; you know, I advised selling out the latter some time ago."

"Yes—yes," she returned impatiently, for she was in no mood to be reminded of the fact. "But can't you suggest something, Mr. Jennings?" she went on pleadingly. "Why, I do not know what it means to be poor like this. I—cannot work; in fact, I should not know what to attempt. Marjorie and I must eat; we have clothes enough to last for some time, but we cannot starve. What are we going to do? Oh, what can we do?" and she actually wrung her hands until the delicate joints cracked.

"How much ready money have you?" Mr. Jennings inquired after a few moments of thought.

"About two hundred dollars," she replied.

The lawyer pursed up his lips, and sat thoughtful again, for it certainly was a dreary outlook for these two luxuriously reared women.

"Are you a good housekeeper—a good manager?" he finally asked.

"No—oh, I don't know! I haven't kept house for years—not since my husband died, and before that I always had servants. I never like it—the care, I mean; and I have been living here, there, and everywhere all these years, while Marjorie was in school. But why do you ask that—what have you in mind?" she concluded with something of interest.

"Well, it occurred to me, since you are so very short of money, that you might, possibly, take a furnished house here in Colorado Springs, and keep boarders——"

"Keep boarders!" interposed Mrs. Ellsworth, with a gasp of dismay, and a shrug of unmistakable disgust.

"But there is lots of money in it," Mr. Jennings pursued. "The prices here are something stupendous, and anybody with a head for managing could make a good living and save a handsome sum every year. You see, there are thousands of consumptive patients sent here from everywhere—a perfect stream pouring in all the time. Many of them are rich, and do not care what they have to pay so they can get where they can breathe, be well cared for, and thus retain their hold on life for a little longer. Now, I know of a good roomy house, owned by a man who wants to go East with his family for a couple of years, at least, and he will let it for a boarding-house, if he can find a reliable party to take it. He wants a hundred and fifty dollars per month, and it must be paid in advance——"

"A hundred and fifty dollars a month!" repeated Mrs. Ellsworth, aghast. "Why, that would be eighteen hundred a year!"

"Exactly; it sounds big, I know, just for rent," said the gentleman, "but it is nicely and completely furnished."

"Even so, I think it is exorbitant—an unheard-of price."

"It is only on a par with everything else here—they all bleed for the last drop. They grasp for the last dollar," said Mr. Jennings, with a shrug of his portly shoulders, "and you'll have to do as the Romans do. Let us make a little estimate, and, perhaps, the undertaking won't seem quite so appalling," he went on, drawing forth a card and a pencil. "The house is large—I think it contains sixteen rooms, and twelve of these could be rented. We will say that these twelve rooms will average four-and-a-half or five dollars a week. Four-and-a-half for one room, for fifty-two weeks, would be two hundred and thirty-four dollars, and twelve times that would be twenty-eight hundred and eight, which would leave a margin of ten hundred and eight dollars after paying your rent, which I call a handsome profit. Of course, there will be some expenses for help, but, even so, you could not fail to do well, for I am told that a good, well-kept house is always full. Then, if you also board your guests, you would charge not less than eight dollars per week—the gentleman is receiving that now—and, with good management, you could not fail to net a handsome sum from your table."

"Oh, but the responsibility would seem like carrying a mountain, to me!" sighed Mrs. Ellsworth gloomily. Then, with a look of mingled cunning and determination gleaming in her eyes, she said: "But I don't see as there is anything else for me to do but to make the trial, if, after looking the house over, I think well of it. Where is the place?"

"It is an attractive residence called Crescent Villa. It is located on high ground, and commands a fine view of the mountains. It is convenient to the North Park and the heart of the town, churches, et cetera, and will, no doubt, be filled to overflowing as soon as it is known as a boarding-house; while, if you set a good table, and give good service, you can command as high prices as anybody. I should advise having everything first-class, for, of course, you would prefer to cater to well-to-do-people."

"Well, I believe I will look at the place," said Mrs. Ellsworth, after thinking the matter over for several minutes; but she sighed heavily as she spoke.

She felt almost crushed at the thought of such an undertaking. But she was like a drowning man clutching at a straw—she felt that there was nothing else left for her to do.

She reasoned that, if she should go back to New York, she had absolutely nothing to live upon, and in that seething metropolis every occupation was overcrowded, and she felt that she would be liable to drift lower and lower, unless she fell back upon her sister-in-law, which she was by no means sure she would be allowed to do. Possibly, Mrs. Sturdyvant might be willing to take Marjorie back with her, when she found to what straits they had been reduced, but she doubted that she would feel that she could give them both a home, and supply their every need, especially as she and Eliza did not always harmonize.

It was now the last week in March, but the party would not probably arrive in Colorado Springs before July or August, for they were going to travel extensively in the East before sailing for the United States, while they would make a tour of California, the Yosemite, and visit other points of interest after arriving in this country; meantime, some provision must be made to meet her own and Marjorie's necessities.

"Very well," Mr. Jennings remarked, in reply to her observation. "We will go around there later. I will see Mr. Allen, with whom I have done considerable business at one time and another, and make an appointment for you. They have a few boarders—Mrs. Allen did not care to fill her house—who would, doubtless, be glad to remain where they are, probably you could also retain the servants, who, as far as I am able to judge, have been well trained."

"When does Mr. Allen wish to vacate?" inquired Mrs. Ellsworth.

"He has been wanting to leave for more than a month; but, as yet, has not been able to find any one to take the house. No doubt he would get out immediately, if you decide to make the venture, and can come to satisfactory terms with him."

Mrs. Ellsworth frowned.

"I think he asks an awful rent," she said. "Don't you suppose you can make better arrangements for me, if I think best to make the plunge?"

"I can, at least, try, and I will do my best for you,"

said the gentleman, rising; "and, if Mr. Allen will be at liberty at four, I will call for you about that time."

"Mamma," said Marjorie, as the door closed upon the man, "surely, you are not equal to such an undertaking! I think it absolutely absurd."

She had been a deeply interested, but chagrined, listener throughout her mother's conversation with her attorney.

She was appalled at the poverty that had so suddently overtaken them; but the thought of having her mother keep a boarding-house to earn their living was a blow to her pride that seemed unendurable.

"Well, maybe I am not; but I can, at least, make the trial—and fail, if I must," Mrs. Ellsworth sharply retorted, for she was in a very irritable frame of mind. "We have got to do something to earn our own bread and butter."

"We?" questioned Marjorie, lifting a glance of innocent surprise at her.

"Certainly. Did you imagine that you would be allowed to sit supinely down, and not put your shoulder to the wheel?"

Marjorie shrugged her pretty shoulders contemptuously, as if thus repudiating all responsibility regarding "the wheel."

"I'm sure, I haven't the slightest idea what I can do—you know, I have never done any work," she remarked.

"Well, then, it is time you began to do something," was the severe retort. "You can at least, learn to make beds, and keep rooms in order—you might wait on table——"

"I wait on table, like a common maid!" gasped the girl indignantly. "I guess not!"

"You will do whatever I tell you to do, Miss Idleness," snapped her mother tartly.

"Perhaps Aunt Eliza will let me go home with her," sighed the girl, with starting tears.

"And leave me here to fight with poverty alone? No, indeed; you've had your day, miss, and now it is high time that you began to do something for yourself and me; if I have got to work for my living, you shall work, also!" cried Mrs. Ellsworth spitefully, and, in a sudden fit of obstinacy, ignoring the fact that, only a few moments previous, she had been saying the same thing to herself.

"I—I won't!" was the sullen rejoinder; "so you can just put that in your pipe and smoke it!" and with this disrespectful and inelegant bit of slang, the girl deliberately turned her back upon her mother, and walked out upon a balcony that overlooked the mountains.

Shortly after four o'clock, Mr. Jennings called, as he had promised, to take Mrs. Ellsworth to "Crescent Villa."

Marjorie sullenly refused to accompany them, and settled herself in a bay window, where she could look off upon the mountains whenever she chose, and with a new novel to occupy the time during her mother's absence.

"Crescent Villa" was within easy walking distance of the hotel, and a stroll of less than ten minutes brought Mrs. Ellsworth and her companion to the place, the grounds of which were well laid out and very attractive.

The house was a handsome, well-built structure, having a broad, roomy veranda on three sides, and which commanded the mountains on one side and a portion of the city from the front.

As they mounted the steps, Mr. Allen, who was watching for their arrival, came forward to meet them, greeting them cordially, and then turned to lead the way into the house.

As he opened the screen door, and was about to enter, a tall, queenly woman, clad in silver gray, with an elaborate fichu of delicate lace, appeared in the doorway, on her way out.

Mr. Allen stepped one side, to allow her to pass.

She smiled as she graciously thanked him, but the next instant stopped short upon the threshold, every atom of color leaving her face, as her startled glance fell upon Mrs. Ellsworth, who was staring, with a horrified look, at her, and at the same time gave vent to a low exclamation of consternation.

CHAPTER IX.

MRS. ALLEN'S VIEWS.

THIS "woman in gray" was Margaret Seymour. She was in perfect health, and had never looked lovelier in her life than at that moment.

She had grown somewhat stouter than of yore, yet not enough so to destroy the symmetrical proportions of her fine figure. She carried herself erect, and with an alertness and freedom of movement which betrayed that she had taken a new and more hopeful lease of life. The hue of a blush rose glowed in her cheeks, her eyes were bright, her whole face animated. She wore a very stylish house-gown of silver-gray cashmere, made en train, with an elaborate lace front, and full frills of the same about her throat and wrists, and, as Marien Ellsworth's keen eyes swept her from head to foot, she could but acknowledge to herself that the woman far surpassed the description which her sister-in-law had given of her.

"Well!" Marien Ellsworth ejaculated, as she was thus suddenly confronted by her old-time rival, and could have bitten her tongue out the next instant, for the ejaculation had escaped her unawares.

Mrs. Seymour, however, after her first start of mingled astonishment and dismay, recovered herself immediately, drew her splendid figure up, with a little added dignity, and, with low "Pardon me"—addressed to Mr. Allen and Mr. Jennings, both of whom had stepped aside to allow her to pass—swept down the veranda to a cozy corner that was enclosed with glass, and where there was a table and chairs, opened a book she had brought out with her, and composedly settled herself to read.

Mrs. Ellsworth flushed hotly with anger, but for that first involuntary start upon beholding her, no one would have suspected that Margaret Seymour had ever laid eyes upon her before, and it galled her inexpressibly to have been thus ignored, especially as she had given expression to her own dismay upon beholding her.

What was Margaret Wilton doing there, she wondered. With her splendid physique, and her buoyant manner, it did not seem possible that she could have come to the place for her health; while she appeared to be in prosperous circumstances, for she was dressed like a princess, in her fine, exquisitely fitting robe, with its rare laces.

These thoughts flashed rapidly through her brain, increasing the irritation that she had been laboring under all day, because of her own misfortunes, and this found vent in a low, mocking laugh, as she followed Mr. Allen inside the house, where she was met by, and introduced to, his wife.

She remained there for nearly an hour, conversing with the owners, and looking the establishment over, and, before the interview terminated, she had decided to take a lease of it for a year, for she had been assured that she could fill it immediately, as the family had already had numberless applications, which they had not cared to avail themselves of, while the owners agreed to vacate at once, giving her possession by the following Monday—four days later.

Before leaving, however Mrs. Ellsworth managed to get Mrs. Allen into a side room, ostensibly to ask her some further questions about servants, furnishings, and so forth, but really for an entirely different purpose.

During their conversation, she observed in a casual way:

"I met a fine-looking woman in gray as I came in; is she one of your guests?"

"Yes, that was Mrs. Seymour. She and her daughter have been with us all winter, and they are most charming people," Mrs. Allen replied. "Miss Seymour is out just now, but she is, if anything, even more beautiful than her mother."

"Do they intend to remain in Colorado Springs indefinitely?" inquired Mrs. Ellsworth, her thin lips compressing themselves ominously, and two perpendicular lines settling in a frown upon her brow.

"I think so. Mrs. Seymour was very frail when she came to us last November, but she began to recuperate almost immediately. She might be said to be in perfect health now; but I think her physician has advised her to remain here through another winter, in order to make assurance doubly sure."

"Well, she cannot remain in this house, if I am to have it!" Mrs Ellsworth asserted, with a decided, acrimonious air and accent.

Mrs. Allen regarded her with astonishment.

"Do you know Mrs. Seymour?" she questioned.

"I used to know her, many years ago," replied Mrs. Ellsworth. Then she added, with a malicious, significant laugh:

"But I have no desire to continue the acquaintance, particularly as I have a young daughter, who will be with me."

"I think I—do not quite understand you, Mrs. Ellsworth!" said Mrs. Allen, flushing slightly. "Both Mrs. Seymour and her daughter came to us well recommended by a Mr. Benyon, of New York City, and they have been charming additions to our household. We have found them cultivated ladies, and most exemplary in every respect."

"Oh, very likely," returned her companion, with a palpable sneer. "It would be for their interest to conduct themselves in a becoming manner; but, allow me to inform you, the woman's name is not Seymour at all, and—her daughter never had a father. Now, you can understand why I refuse to allow them to remain in the house," she concluded, with a malicious gleam in her eyes, which betrayed a bitter and relentless grudge against the one of whom she was speaking.

Mrs. Allen had grown absolutely colorless, as she listened to these vile insinuations, and an expression of mingled indignation and pain gleamed in her usually mild eyes.

"Really, Mrs. Ellsworth, I am very sorry that you have told me this," she observed in a tone of unmistakable coldness. "The deportment of both Mrs. Seymour and her daughter has been irreproachable ever since they came to us, and even if there has been a —a mistake in their past—which I cannot believe—it certainly does not seem kind or charitable to bring it up against them here and now."

"Oh, well, those things are sure to come out, first or last," retorted Marian Ellsworth, with an angry toss of her head, for she did not relish the reproofs she had received.

"Yes, it seems so," replied Mrs. Allen, with ironical significance. Then she continued in a tone of sincere regret: "And what a pity it is that people are so much more eager to circulate all the evil they hear and know of others, rather than to shield them, or tell of their virtues. But, Mrs. Ellsworth, I earnestly hope that you will speak of this to no one else; for, notwithstanding what you have told me, I firmly believe Mrs. and Miss Seymour to be most estimable ladies."

"All the same, I will not have them here," persisted Mrs. Ellsworth, with something of sharpness, for she was thoroughly enraged at the plain speaking to which she had been compelled to listen. "One must protect one's own reputation, and I will not have my daughter contaminated by their presence in my house."

"Of course, I can have nothing to say regarding that; you are at liberty to choose your own guests, if you take Crescent Villa," was the icy reply; "but" drawing herself up, as if from a sense of conscious superiority, "I have this to say of the ladies whom you have so traduced: I feel honored to have had them in my family, and should continue so to feel, if I were to remain here."

Mrs. Ellsworth began to think it was time to beat a retreat, for she was getting decidedly the worst of the argument. She had been made to feel that she had done a mean thing, even if her gossip had not been false from first to last.

She glanced at her watch, and said it was getting toward dinner-time, and she would like a few moments' further conversation with Mr. Allen before she went away.

Mrs. Allen accompanied her to the parlor, where the two gentlemen were discussing politics, and then, with a feeling of disgust for the woman, quietly withdrew to her own room, devoutly hoping, that what she had been told regarding the Seymours would go no farther.

She was destined to be disappointed, however, for, even if it had not been Marien Ellsworth's determination to drive the Seymours from the house, and the city, if possible, her miserable tale would have soon been noised abroad.

There was another guest in the house—a fashionable spinster, of uncertain age—who never allowed anything to escape her sharp eyes and ears, if she could help it. She had been sitting on the piazza, just outside an open window, near which Mrs. Allen and Mrs. Ellsworth had stood while conversing, and had overheard every word that was said, though she herself could not be seen.

She watched the departure of the mischief-maker with no little curiosity and interest, since she was soon to be the proprietor of the establishment. Then she gathered up the papers she had been reading, and sailed, with a consequential air, into the house, almost bursting with the delicious scandal she had heard, and passing Mrs. Seymour on her way without a word, or even a nod of recognition.

Before dinner was served, every one in the house had been regaled with an embellished account of Mrs. Seymour's past and Miss Seymour's doubtful parentage.

By noon of the following day, neighbors had the story, whereupon the social atmosphere immediately fell to the freezing-point, and averted looks and icy manners greeted Helen and her mother on every hand.

By afternoon, matters had reached such a crisis, Mrs. Seymour sought Mrs. Allen, and inquired if she could enlighten her regarding the meaning of it all.

In a kind and sympathetic manner, Mrs. Allen frankly told her just what Mrs. Ellsworth had said.

"But," she added, with a sigh, "I am at a loss to understand how her wretched gossip has become public property so soon, for I have not repeated a word she told me."

"I think I understand it," Mrs. Seymour observed. "Miss Lampson was sitting on the piazza, on that side of the house; she must have overheard something, if not all, of what was said, for she went in just as soon as Mrs. Ellsworth left, and, when she passed me, she held her head very high, and ignored me entirely."

"Ah! That accounts for it, for I remember we were

standing near an open window," replied Mrs. Allen; then continued: "I saw at once that the woman had a mean spite against you, and I could not believe what she told me. Is it not contemptible that people will so eagerly seize a morsel of scandal, and flaunt it broadcast for others, as evil-minded as themselves, to feast upon?"

Mrs. Seymour was white to her lips and a look of anguish was in her eyes.

She did not care so much for herself, but to have Helen subjected to the contempt and frowns of cruel scandal-mongers, and a stain falsely fastened upon her birth, touched her in a very tender spot.

"It is true that Mrs. Ellsworth knew me many years ago," she told Mrs. Allen. "She was my chum at school, and at that time my dearest friend. Afterward, when she was homeless and penniless, I took her into my own home, and supplied her every need. Then she became madly jealous of me, and laid a plot to ruin my life. What she has told you is true, in a certain way, and yet as false as it can possibly be—if you can comprehend such a paradoxical statement."

She smiled, with some bitterness, as she said this; then after a moment, she resumed:

"It is true that my name is not Seymour. I assumed it in order to conceal my identity after the terrible sorrow that came upon me through that woman, and Helen never had a father, in one sense of the word, for she was born after I—left my home. But"—with a proud uplifting of her regal head—"I am a legally married woman. Helen's birth is above suspicion of reproach, and, Mrs. Allen, because of your exceeding charity and kindness in this matter, I am going to show you what no one else, save my husband, myself and the clergyman who married me, has ever seen—my marriage certificate. But I must ask you not to disclose the names you will read there, for even Helen does not know them."

As she concluded, she drew a small silken bag from her bosom, and, taking a folded paper from it, she passed it to her companion.

"Certainly; I will never betray your confidence—you may trust me implicitly, dear Mrs. Seymour," Mrs. Allen heartily returned, as she took the document and read it carefully through. "I did not need this to assure me that you yourself are above reproach," she smilingly observed, as she passed the paper back to her; then added inquiringly: "Of course you will allow me to contradict that wretched gossip, even though I may not mention names?"

"Certainly, I would like you to do so, for Helen's sake. But, under the circumstances, I think I will seek another home immediately. Of course, I could not remain here, with Marien Ellsworth for my landlady, even if she had not asserted that she would not have me," Mrs. Seymour observed, a crimson spot burning on either cheek.

"No, indeed, I would not have you stay for anything, for I am disgusted with the people who have given you the cold shoulder on the strength of what a perfect stranger has said, after having known and lived in the house with you for so many months," spiritedly replied Mrs. Allen. "If the lease had not been made out and signed last night, and the first payment made, I believe I should urge Mr. Allen to cancel it, for I feel confident that the woman is a vindictive mischief-maker, and I should not be surprised if she continued to try to make trouble for you."

"I have not a doubt of it myself," said Mrs. Seymour, with a sigh.

"Never mind, my friend,' said her companion cheerfully. "Let me advise you to pay no attention to her; don't let her drive you out of the place; stay quietly here, go on the even tenor of your way, and those who know you, and whose esteem is worth retaining will still be glad to own you and Helen as friends, while it will take but a very little while for people to make their estimate of a woman who descends to falsehood and such petty measures to injure you, and regard her with the contempt she deserves."

"Thank you, dear Mrs. Allen, for your sympathy and kindly counsel," said Mrs. Seymour, with starting tears, adding: "But I had already made up my mind not to be driven away; and, now, can you advise me where to go to find a comfortable and pleasant home for Helen and myself? I do not expect to find a second Mrs. Allen, however," she concluded, smiling through her tears.

"Yes, I can. Some people are leaving Mrs. Forsyth's to-day. She keeps a fine house, and is very particular who she admits to her household. I will go out, right now, to see if I cannot secure the vacated rooms for you," her hostess returned, with animation.

"But how will it be when Mrs. Forsyth comes to hear Mrs. Ellsworth's garbled version of my history?" suggested Mrs. Seymour, with a sigh.

"We will forestall the woman," was the spirited response. "I will tell Mrs. Forsyth something of what you have related to me, and, as we have been friends for years, I am sure she will be governed by my recommendation, and be your stanch ally and defender."

The good woman proceeded at once to put her resolution into execution, and, upon her return, informed Mrs. Seymour that there were two delightful rooms at her disposal in the home of her friend, Mrs. Forsyth, and the next forenoon found Helen and her mother pleasantly located in their new home.

Mrs. Allen was burdened with many cares and responsibilities during the next two or three days in preparing to vacate her house; but she neglected no opportunity to contradict the gossip which she heard on every hand regarding her recent guests.

It must be confessed, however, she met with rather indifferent success in her kind endeavors.

"Oh, well, but that is only one side of the story," said Miss Lampson, the spinster, who had been so diligent in circulating the news she had overheard, and whom Mrs. Allen took especial pains to interview. "I am always very charitable toward people, and like to believe the best of everybody," she continued, with a virtuous and superior air; "but, you know, 'there is never any smoke without some fire.'"

"I have told you that there was a semblance of truth in what that woman said; but it was distorted beyond all recognition," returned Mrs. Allen, with a touch of impatience that she rarely displayed. "I have told you that Mrs. Seymour showed me the certificate of her marriage; and do you not see there can be no foundation for that malicious statement that she was no wife, and that Helen was fatherless?"

"Well, possibly not," was the somewhat skeptical response; "and yet it would be a very easy matter for a person to get a bogus certificate made out. That doesn't prove anything to me. What did you say the name of the man was to whom she claims to have been married?" she insinuatingly inquired.

"I did not say," coldly replied Mrs. Allen. "That is a point upon which I do not feel at liberty to speak, since Mrs. Seymour showed me the paper in confidence."

"O—h!" observed the spinster, with lifted eyebrows and dilated nostrils. "So the husband is nameless, as well as the girl! That looks as if there was some cause for the smoke. However, the new landlady doubtless knows all about it, and I'll have the whole story out of her yet. I always do manage to get at the bottom of anything, when I set about it."

"Oh, Miss Lampson, don't you think that Mrs. Seymour and her daughter have conducted themselves in a way to command the esteem and respect of every one ever since they have been in the house? I'm sure you cultivated their friendship as if you appreciated it; and don't you think that entitles them to the benefit of the doubt of Mrs. Ellsworth's motives in circulating malicious reports, especially as nobody knows anything about her?"

"Um—yes; Mrs. Seymour—I suppose we shall have to continue to call her that, since we do not know her real name—has seemed a very estimable lady, and Helen certainly has a very taking way with her; but —somehow, I always suspect people who are excessively exemplary, and have often found that they have a past that won't bear looking into."

"Well, I have found that people who are so suspicious of others sometimes have a past that won't bear looking into," retorted Mrs. Allen, her temper, for the moment, getting the better of her.

"Allow me to inquire what you mean, Mrs. Allen?" said Miss Lampson in a high-and-mighty tone, but with a gleam of anxiety in her eyes.

"I was speaking in general terms," was the cold response.

"Ah, if that was all, very well," said the spinster, as, turning away, she sought her own room, but deeply chagrined because she could not ascertain the real name of Mrs. Seymour, and vowing that she would worm the secret from Mrs. Ellsworth, or "pump her dry," as she expressed it, at the earliest possible opportunity.

"And she calls that being 'charitable!' She 'always wants to believe the best of everybody!'" exclaimed Mrs. Allen in disgust, as the woman disappeared.

"Well, then, deliver me from all such charity; but I believe the day will come when both she and that Ellsworth woman will get their pay."

And it did, although they kept the "fire" burning and the "smoke" spreading for many weeks.

CHAPTER X.

HELEN'S FATHER.

THE Allens left Colorado Springs on Monday morning.

The same day, Mrs. Ellsworth took possession of Crescent Villa, and, from the hour that she entered its portals, a new régime was instituted in the domestis arrangements of the establishment. The woman was bitter to her heart's core because of her losses, her disappointments, the change in her position, and the relentless fate that had decreed that she must work for her living, and she hated work of any sort.

Instead of the bland and smiling society woman, who had always exerted herself to please others, instead of being punctilious in the observance of all the courtesies of life, she seemed to have suddenly become hard and sour. There was a discontented, sullen look on her face, two deeply indented perpendicular lines upon her frowning brow, and a compression about her lips that indicated some deeply laid purpose.

That purpose was to make the utmost of her opportunities to gather into her purse every penny that she could extort from those with whom she came in contact, until she could see her way clear toward bettering her condition in some other way; possibly, by an advantageous marriage with some successful mining speculator, or business man, she cared not which or who, so that she could get rid of the yoke of poverty.

Marjorie, also, was changed. She was suave and agreeable enough toward those guests in the house to whom she was attracted; but, to those whom she did not like, she was often pert and supercilious. Toward her mother, who insisted that she should lend a helping hand in various ways, she had grown disrespectful and irritable, until frequent clashings occurred between them, even in the presence of their guests.

Marjorie and Helen had not met, although several weeks had elapsed since the Ellsworths came to the city; but one day Marjorie returned from down-town, whither she had gone upon an errand, and excitedly informed her mother that she had seen Helen and her mother, riding in a stylish turnout, with some very swell people, although they had not observed her.

Mrs. Ellsworth saw, from her manner, that she was still fond of the girl, and emphatically forbade her ever to speak to her, even if they should meet—she would have no inter-communication between the families.

"I shall speak to her, if I choose!" the girl impudently retorted, and with an air of sullen defiance; but she had no intention of coming in contact with Helen, if she could avoid it, for her own sense of wrongdoing made her ashamed to meet her.

And yet there were times when she yearned, from the depths of her heart, for the sweet, pure girl, and for the ennobling influence of her presence.

She often wondered how the Seymours happened to be there; what it meant that Helen was not married, after all, as Mr. Lancaster had told her she was going to be, and what the outcome of it all would be.

Now and then, she showed traces of good blood, when she happened to hear the reputation of the Seymours assailed.

For instance, in tilts with the much-in-evidence Miss Lampson, who regaled every newcomer to the house—which, by the way, was now always full, as had been prophesied—with the history of the two ladies, and their expulsion from Crescent Villa, for Mrs. Ellsworth claimed that she had "demanded their rooms, because of their questionable reputation."

On one occasion, the girl was lazily swinging in a hammock on the veranda, while some gossip of this kind was going on. She stood it as long as she could; then lifting her head from her pillow, she turned her blazing eyes upon the woman.

"I think it absolutely shameful to be continually backbiting them!" she cried. "I know all about Helen Seymour, and nobody has a right to say one word against her—she is as lovely as she can be."

"Well, Marjorie, there is no reason for your becoming so excited over this matter," pompously returned the spinster. "I grant that Helen Seymour is a pretty girl—an awfully pretty girl; but——"

"There is no 'but' that can be said against her!" pertly interposed Marjorie, and mimicing the woman's inflection to perfection. "She is the sweetest, dearest, most generous-hearted girl in the world; and her mother—well, if all you people would just stop your gossiping long enough to study that woman's character, you would be improving your time to better advantage!"

"And you would do well to cultivate a little more civility, Miss Impertinence," retorted Miss Lampson, with a very red face.

I suppose I would," observed Marjorie severely; "but, if you please, I'll have my say out first, for I'm quite stirred up over hearing those really good people so slandered. Why the Seymours have a summer home in the Adirondacks, where I go to visit my aunt, Mrs. Sturdyvant, sometimes, and everybody there thinks the world of them."

"Probably nothing is known of Mrs. Seymour's—or whatever her name be—history there; however, your mother is responsible for the story, so suppose you turn your quills upon her in the future." And, with this arrow from her own quiver, shot with a withering glance at Marjorie, the ruffled spinster went into the house.

Her curiosity had been aroused to the highest pitch regarding the mystery about the Seymours, and several times she had tried to sound Mrs. Ellsworth upon the subject, but the woman had told all she cared to of that episode in which she had so disgracefully figured in her youth; hints and insinuations served her purpose as well as anything, and so the "pumping act" had not been at all successful.

"Never mind," this queen of idlers and busybodies would say to herself upon these occasions; "I'll have the whole story one of these days. I never yet set about finding out about people that I did not accomplish it some way."

She felt it her duty to keep her eye upon the Seymours, and so, one day, she went to call upon Mrs. Forsyth, with whom she had some acquaintance, both ladies attending the same church. She was in her most affable mood, and the call was, apparently, very agreeable to both parties until Miss Lampson was about to take her departure.

"So you have the Seymours with you?" she casually observed, as she abstracted a card from her case and laid it upon a table.

"Yes; and how sorry you must have been to lose them from your house—they are such delightful people!" Mrs. Forsyth returned, but with a wicked sparkle in her eyes.

"Y—es, they seemed to be very nice," rejoined Miss Lampson, with a doubtful intonation; "but we learned that their past history has rather a high flavor."

"Ah!"

"Of course, it is none of my affair, and I am the last person in the world to say anything against anybody," the woman went on, but not quite liking the tone her companion had employed; "but, as you are dependent upon your business, I thought it would be no more than fair that you should be warned, lest the reputation of your house should suffer."

"Thank you for your good intentions," suddenly interposed her hostess suavely, but with a slight emphasis on the adjective, which caused her listener to flush hotly; "but, really, I do not fear that the reputation of my house will ever suffer through the Seymours. They are favorites with every one here; and, as for their history—well, we all have had episodes in our lives, you know."

Miss Lampson was politely bowed out, but there was a very queer look on her face as she went on her way.

"What did she mean by 'episodes,' I wonder!" she muttered to herself, with an uncomfortable shrug of her shoulders.

Poor Marjorie was very wretched during these days. She grew to hate her life more and more as time went on, for Mrs. Ellsworth was developing more of a sordid, grasping disposition with every day, a determination to extort the uttermost farthing, together with an oppression and grinding down of her servants, that was entirely at variance with her hitherto free-and-easy manner of living.

She hated, too, the servitude and work which were required of her, for her mother refused to keep sufficient help to do all that was necessary, and thus she was obliged to perform certain duties every day that were exceedingly obnoxious to her.

Thus there was gradually taking form in her mind a determination to get away from it all, by some means, and at the earliest possible opportunity.

"Oh, if I could only go home with Aunt Eliza!" she sighed, again and again; and then a sense of shame, in view of wishing to desert her mother for a life of ease and supine dependence, leaving her to fight out her battle with poverty alone, would rush over her, and she would feel mean and miserable.

"No; I will find somebody who has plenty of money, and will get married; then I can give mamma a home, and she need not work at all," she finally resolved, though with a feeling of grim despair, as she thought of Rob, for she had really and truly poured upon him all the love she was capable of bestowing upon any human being.

She was dreading the arrival of the party in Colorado Springs, for she told herself that Rob and Helen would be sure to meet, and then everything would be explained between the lovers.

Of course her curiosity regarding Helen and her interrupted marriage would almost get the better of her, and she would feel that she must see her friend, and find out all about it, in spite of her mother's prohibition.

But always at such times a realization of her own unworthiness and wrongdoing, her deception and falsehoods, her treachery toward those who had been kind and sincere friends to her, would so humiliate her that she instinctively shrank from an interview with them.

Helen, on her part, was grieved at the existing state of affairs, for she had really been very fond of Marjorie, and she would have been glad to renew their friendship in spite of the barrier which had arisen between them after the girl's confession of love for Rob.

She, also, had wondered what could have brought Mrs. Ellsworth to Colorado Springs, for she had supposed them to be still traveling with the party which Mr. Lancaster and Rob had joined. She often asked herself if it could be possible that they had returned earlier than they had intended, and if the Ellsworths had stopped off at that point for reasons of their own, while the others went on. It was very evident that they had met with reverses, or they would not now be keeping a boarding-house. And where was Mrs. Sturdyvant, whom she knew had been regarded as a wealthy woman? Why had she not opened her heart and home to them? Thus it will be perceived that Helen's curiosity had also been aroused, and, had it not been for the wretched reports which Mrs. Ellsworth had circulated—although Mrs. Seymour had kept the worst from her—she would have been tempted to seek Marjorie herself.

But one day she overheard some people discussing these very reports, while she was waiting for some change in a store, and she went home to her mother in a great state of excitement and indignation.

"I cannot understand it, mamma!" she exclaimed. "I cannot understand why the woman would say such false things! What cause can she have—what right to assert anything so disgraceful? Why, it actually makes my blood boil to think of it—to have our good name so assailed, when there is not a word of truth in the story!"

Mrs. Seymour felt that the time had come when she must tell her daughter something of the truth, for there was no knowing to what lengths Marien Ellsworth would go, and she wished her to be prepared for whatever revelations might come later. And yet she could not tell her all—ah, no! She must never learn the name of her father, if she could avoid telling it, for she never could allow the two to meet and recognize each other as father and daughter! Helen was hers alone, by every right, moral and divine, and she meant to keep her thus always.

"Helen," she gravely observed, in reply to her excited remarks, "do you remember that, when you told me of your acquaintance with Marjorie Ellsworth, I said I wondered if she could be the child of Marien Waldbridge?"

"Yes, mamma; I also remember how queerly you spoke of her—almost as if you hated her."

"Yes; and no doubt I did manifest some such feeling for the moment," replied Mrs. Seymour, flushing as she recalled the fact, " for I had abundant reason; and now I have come to feel that it is only right I should tell you that Mrs. Ellsworth is Marien Waldbridge."

"Mamma, can that be possible?" And she is that 'false friend' of which you have already told me?" queried Helen, astonished.

"Yes; although I would have been glad never to have had to speak her name again—in fact, to have buried all the past with which she is associated in oblivion."

"You need not tell me anything more, dear, if it pains you to talk about it," said Helen considerately.

"I think it will, perhaps, be best for you to understand something of her history, and why she is trying to injure us in the way she is doing," returned Mrs. Seymour, after a thoughtful pause, during which she had been almost tempted to take Helen at her word, for she shrank sensitively from the task before her. "The impression which she has been giving people about us, the insinuations which she has been sowing broadcast, while absolutely false, as far as involving any disgrace on our part, are, nevertheless, in a way founded upon fact."

"Mamma!"

"Listen, dear," interposed Mrs. Seymour, checking her with a gesture; " you must let me tell it in my own way, and you must be content with what I tell you, for there are some things that must remain a secret in my own heart—things that I cannot talk about—that withered my youth, and bereft me of my greatest joy, my highest hopes in life. Marien Waldbridge was my roommate for three years while we were in the boarding-school, where I had been sent to complete my education. The year before she was to graduate, her father failed in business, then suddenly died, leaving the girl an orphan, and absolutely penniless. She appeared to be heart-broken because she could not go on with her school, and, as my father had left me a comfortable little sum, I told Marien that I would be responsible for the expenses of that last year, for I expected to be married as soon as I left school to a wealthy gentleman, and felt that I could well afford to be generous to that extent, while she would be thus prepared to teach, and earn her own living. We graduated at the same time, and, as she had no home to go to for her long vacation, I wrote, asking my Aunt Wesley—my mother's half-sister, with whom I was to remain until my marriage —if she would receive my friend, also. Cordial permission was given. A month later, I was married, and Marien was my maid of honor. I then invited her to come to me until she could find a good position as a teacher. She lived with me for more than a year, making no effort whatever to get anything to do, and, although I could not fail to feel that she was encroaching upon our hospitality, I treated her like an own sister, and provided liberally for her every need, for my husband was generous as a prince, and gratified my every whim. Well, Helen—I cannot begin to tell you all—that girl betrayed me in the basest possible way; it was she who, after worming herself into my husband's confidence, made him believe that I was unfaithful to him——"

"Oh, what ingratitude! She was, indeed a 'false friend?'" exclaimed Helen at this point.

"Yes, dear," continued her mother, with white lips,

"it was she who encouraged that other, of whom I have told you, to believe that I was unhappy with my husband, regretted my choice, and would be glad to be free. It was she who planned to admit him to my private sitting-room, and then, when he was in the midst of his passionate avowals, in which he assumed that I wished to escape from the life I was leading, she managed, by a clever maneuver, to have my husband walk in upon us, having heard, as he believed, enough to incriminate us both. When I tried to argue and explain, he would not listen to a word of defense from me; he said he had heard enough with his own ears to convince him of all he cared to know; no man would presume to make such proposals to a married woman if he had not had plenty of encouragement to do so—and so on. I cannot rehearse the scene," sighed the woman, wearily.

"I was so crushed, so heart-broken and humiliated because of his lack of confidence in me," she presently resumed—"I was so wounded, and offended—for I was proud and passionate, as well as he—that, as I have told you before, I left him and my beautiful home, and —Helen, I—have lived alone ever since."

"Mamma! What do you mean?" exclaimed the girl, sitting suddenly erect, and shocked to her soul, as, from her mother's peculiar intonation, and the wording of that last sentence, a suspicion of the truth flashed upon her. "Mamma—then my father didn't die! But you told me——"

"Yes, dear, I told you that I lost him before you were born. I allowed you to believe him dead—he was dead to me—for I could not bear to have your life blighted by a knowledge of the true nature of my trouble, while I knew that you would be ceaselessly tormented with a yearning desire to find and know him. Sometimes I have felt that I had done wrong to keep the truth from you, as well as the knowledge of your existence from him. But I felt that you belonged exclusively to me. I never could part with you, and I was too proud, and obstinate, and selfish to tell him, and let him come to see you, and win your love."

"And—and is he living still?" queried Helen in a scarcely audible voice.

"Yes—or was less than two years ago."

"Who is he? What is his name—the name that rightly belongs to you and me? Where does he live?" cried Helen in eager tones.

"Those are questions, Helen, that I do not wish to answer," said Mrs. Seymour, with firm-set lips, "and you must not press me to do so. The past is past; nothing can change it now, and I am so bound up in you that I cannot bear that you should ever meet him. It can do you no good to learn the name which you assert rightly belongs to us; it would only make you restless and miserable. The one we have borne in the past will do well enough for us in the future."

"But——"

"My darling, you must not press me upon this point," interposed Mrs. Seymour almost sharply; "and now, let us drop the subject, for I cannot talk more about it. I have only told you this much to show you how wickedly Marien Ellsworth has perverted the truth. In a certain sense, I have no right to the name I bear, and you never had a father; she has taken that way to smirch our reputation, and drive us out of the place; but she knows that the impression she has given is as false as false can be."

"Well, tell me this, mamma," Helen began eagerly. Then she sank back weakly, as light suddenly flashed upon her. "Ah, but you do not need to—I know already!" she sighed.

"What is it that you know, dear?" questioned her

mother, while she searched her face, with a rapidly beating heart and clouded eyes.

"I was going to ask you if that other man, who made such dishonorable proposals to you, is still living; but, of course, I know; though, for the moment, I forgot—and, oh!" she went on, with flaming eyes and crimson cheeks; "I think he did you as great a wrong as that woman who plotted to ruin you! What right had he to annoy and insult you in any such way, while you were the wife of another man? Why could he not have left you alone? Oh, he has not only ruined your life, but he has ruined mine twice over!" she concluded, her thoughts reverting to the telegram and letter from Mr. Lancaster, which she still had in her possession.

"Oh, what are you speaking, Helen—what do you mean by saying that he has ruined your life twice over?" her mother inquired, a look of perplexity overspreading her face.

"Why—why," faltered the excited girl, with a sudden start, as she remembered that she had never known anything about the letter and telegram, "I—of course, since he was the cause of all the wretchedness you have known, and was, in that way, the means of depriving me of my father, he has been guilty of a double wrong to me, and—I will never forgive him—never—never!" she concluded passionately, and then she burst into a terrible fit of weeping.

CHAPTER XI.

HELEN AND MARJORIE.

MRS. SEYMOUR had flushed a sudden crimson while Helen was speaking, and then the color had died almost as quickly out of her face, leaving her startlingly pale.

She sat for a moment or two regarding the weeping girl, a look of inexpressible sadness, mingled with something of perplexity, in her eyes.

At length, she observed in a gentle tone:

"Helen, I have never known you to manifest so much of temper, and vindictiveness before! Dear, it was that unforgiving spirit that was my bane," she went on, with a sigh; "if I had not been quite so rash and headstrong—if I had waited a few days, thus giving my husband's anger and jealousy a chance to cool, his reason and affection an opportunity to reassert themselves, I feel sure that he would have regretted his hasty judgment of me and that we might to-day, perhaps, have been a united and happy family. For many, many years I cherished that unchristian disposition; but, since I have been so ill, I have found my bitterness disappearing, in a measure. I have realized that I was not wholly blameless regarding that hasty separation. I left my husband without a word of warning; I left him desolate and alone in the lovely home which he had taken such infinite pains and pleasure in preparing for me, upon which he spared no expense to gratify my tastes——"

"But he should have had more confidence in you; he had no right to believe you unfaithful to him, when you had chosen him from all the world to be your husband," interposed Helen, who could not bear to have her mother blame herself.

"Yes, I agree with you there, dear; he should, at least, have listened to my defense. I know that he was unreasonable, and I felt myself irreparably wronged because he did not trust me, in spite of the apparent evidence against me. And yet, looking back, I can see that the plot had been so cleverly laid and worked up that almost any man would, under the excitement of the moment, have believed that his wife had been very indiscreet, to say the least. But his mistakes do not excuse mine," Mrs. Seymour continued, with a regretful sigh; "and, since I have had so much time to think, I have tried to look at matters from his standpoint, as well as from my own, and I have come to feel that I, the wife, should have exercised more patience and forbearance."

"Mamma, would you forgive and take him back to-day, if the opportunity should offer?" questioned Helen, lifting her tear-stained face, and regarding her companion earnestly, even yearningly.

Again the woman flushed, and a spasm of unutterable agony contracted her sensitive mouth.

"My darling, that is a hard question," she said. "A year and a half ago, I should have given you a positive 'No!' but, after having been down so low into the 'valley of the shadow,' I have often felt that I would like to forgive as I would be forgiven, before I go hence. As for the 'taking back,' that is another matter, and, perchance, it would not be for me alone to decide; for, after years of separation, and pursuing entirely different paths in life, it might not be an easy matter to gather up and unite the broken threads of our life again."

"Mamma, I wish you would tell me my father's name," pleaded Helen, with a troubled look.

"Ah, I feared you would be unsettled, if you once learned the fact that he still lives!" said her mother regretfully. "But do not press me, dear; I cannot tell you—at least, not at present. Some time perhaps, I may find courage, but not now."

An expression of disappointment swept over the girl's fair face at this refusal; but, having always been considerate of her mother's wishes, she quietly yielded the point, and, a few moments later, arose and left the room, seeking her own.

As she closed and locked her door—for she felt that she must be left alone to master the conflict of emotions that was raging within—she burst again into tears.

"I will never forgive him!" she sobbed; "that bad, unprincipled man! To think that he should have been the means of driving her from her lovely home and husband, thus depriving me of a father's loving care and protection, and then adding to that sin this other of separating Rob and me! Oh, Rob! Rob!"

That last pathetic cry betrayed the continuous, though hitherto voiceless, yearning of her wounded heart—a yearning that was growing stronger and more intense with every passing day, especially since the Ellsworths had settled in Colorado Springs, and she had instinctively felt that all was at an end between him and Marjorie.

We left Mrs. Seymour and her daughter located, for the summer previous, in a comfortable farmhouse in Yonkers. There the invalid had begun, after a week or two, to slowly recuperate, and, by the first of October, had gained considerable strength and several pounds of flesh.

Her cough was much better, and she began to show a tinge of color in her hollow cheeks.

But her physician was emphatic in his assertions

that it would never do for her to remain in that rigorous climate during the winter.

He strongly advised her to go South, or—what he said would be a hundredfold better—take a trip to Colorado, and remain in that high altitude for a year, if she felt that she could afford the expense of such a journey, and rest.

"I feel sure that I can promise you a return of perfect health, if you will do as I advise," he had said, while discussing the matter with her. "Your lungs are not diseased, but they are weak, and could not endure the slightest relapse. You have begun to rally, and are doing well, but you will certainly lose all you have gained, and run the risk of even worse, if you try to remain here for the coming winter. I do not like, as a rule, to send patients like you South, for the climate, though milder than ours, is enervating; but it is better than no change at all. Colorado is the place for you to get well in, and I wish you could see your way clear to go there."

"We will go there," Helen had at once declared, with an assertiveness that made her mother smile.

Indeed, she had assumed an air of authority and of manager in general throughout her illness that had been very helpful and restful to her.

But the spirit of economy within her took alarm at once at this bold assertion.

"My dear, I am sure you can have no idea of the expense of idly spending a winter in Colorado!" she observed.

"Well, but our summer here has been very inexpensive," the girl responded, "and I am sure we can afford to spend enough to give you the trip the doctor wishes you to take. Suppose it even takes half, or two-thirds, of what we have, you will then have a good bunch of money left with which to begin business again on your return. What do we care, mamma, so that you have your health back? And then, besides, it will be such a delightful experience; you know that you and I have never seen very much of this grand world of ours."

Her arguments appealed both to Mrs. Seymour's judgment and inclination, so the matter was settled, and the last week in October found them en route for that noted resort for invalids, Colorado Springs, where they were fortunate enough to secure rooms and board at Crescent Villa with good, kind Mrs. Allen, who received only a limited number into her house, exerted herself to make her guests feel happy and at home, and here they remained until Marien Ellsworth came, like a bird of ill omen, and drove them from their comfortable nest, and where Mrs. Seymour had steadily improved from the hour of her arrival. She felt so nearly well and like herself that, as spring approached, she began to talk of going home to resume business; but, after exchanging letters with her physician, she decided that she would remain until her year was out, and perhaps, through the winter.

It was a great trial to both Helen and her mother to have Mrs. Allen go away, because they had grown very fond of her, and had found a delightful home with her; but Mrs. Forsythe's house proved to be very attractive, and the woman herself—her sympathies having been enlisted in their behalf—a stanch friend to them.

But their enemy, together with certain other mischief-makers, had done their work so cunningly and effectually that many people, who had previously been most cordial and friendly in their intercourse with them, began to regard them askance, and to give them the cold shoulder.

"Never mind," Mrs. Seymour said cheerfully to Helen, when, one day, the girl expressed her indignation at the treatment to which they were being subjected, and against Mrs. Ellsworth and Miss Lampson, in particular, for so industriously and persistently circulating the false reports; "we know that we are all right—that we are simply being subjected to unjust and vulgar persecution. I would far rather be in our position than in that of those who are trying to injure us. In fact, I find my heart full of pity for such people as inhabit most of the ordinary boarding-houses; they lead such idle, aimless lives that they simply drop into the habit of gossip, and so literally feed upon scandal, and demoralize themselves."

"All the same, they manage to make one feel decidedly uncomfortable," said Helen, flushing over the remembrance of the lofty air and direct cut which she had recently received from Miss Lampson.

"We will hold ourselves above it, dear, and everything will work itself right with time," was the comforting response from her mother. Then she added: "I am getting so well and strong, I believe we will go home at the end of one year, after all, when we will resume our old, quiet, happy life, and forget all about it. We will not go before—even though I feel perfectly able—for it shall not be said that we were driven away."

So they went on the even tenor of their way, as good Mrs. Allen had advised them, in spite of averted looks and suggestive shrugs; and thus the spring and a portion of the summer slipped by, and the time of the great festival of the year—the Flower Carnival—drew nigh.

Meantime, Marjorie, with an ever-increasing desire to escape the life she was leading, met a young physician, Dr. Black by name, and was receiving his constant attentions.

"A fine young man," was the recommendation of

the gentleman who had introduced him to her, and who had employed him in his family upon several occasions. "He has an excellent practise, which is bound to increase, and, already, has an income of three or four hundred a month."

The young practitioner in question certainly conducted himself in the most exemplary manner, was devoted to his fair charmer, visiting at Crescent Villa every day, and, while he claimed to be most particular not to neglect his "large and growing practise," found many opportunities to drive her about in his nobby turnout, and take her to various points of interest. Finally, there came a day when he declared his love for her, and asked her to become his wife.

Marjorie could not, at first, decide her fate. Her heart was still very sore over her recent disappointment, and her yearning for Rob, but, knowing how hopeless was her love for him, she felt that she could not afford to neglect a good opportunity to be well settled in life.

She was conscious that she did not, and never could, love the doctor as she had loved Rob, yet she did not dislike him, and thought, perhaps, they would get on very well together. He seemed to be a gentleman, was courteous and affable in manner, intelligent, and apparently, as far as she could judge, a man of good habits. Mrs. Ellsworth, as well as Marjorie, was attracted by the "large and growing practise," thought it would be a good match for the girl—with whom she quarreled more and more frequently—and so manifested her approval of the proposed alliance. From the first, she had taken special pains to let it be known that Marjorie was the declared heiress of her father's sister, Mrs. Sturdyvant, who was a widow possessing a fortune of at least a hundred thousand dollars.

But Marjorie would not decide the all-important

question until she heard from her aunt—to whom she had written all the facts of the case—and received her sanction to, or, at least, her advice regarding the union.

The party had arrived in San Francisco when this letter was received, but would not reach Colorado Springs until some time in August—some five or six weeks later.

Mrs. Sturdyvant replied that she thought everything appeared to be most propitious for her future, if her information regarding the doctor was reliable, and she was sure she cared enough for him to pass her life with him. Under these circumstances, she could give them her heartiest blessing, and would set them up at housekeeping, when they were ready to be married; that they might choose the house they wished to live in, and she would furnish it handsomely for them, and also provide Marjorie with a generous wedding trousseau.

This certainly seemed to be a very promising beginning, and Marjorie, thinking that she might, perhaps, be able to meet Rob, upon his arrival, with more self-possession and sang-froid, if she was engaged, gave her promise to the doctor, and they set the date for their marriage for the middle of October.

A few miles from the city, there was a delightful resort, known as Broadmore, where was located a large hotel, with several cottages and a fine casino.

Here, during the summer, an excellent orchestra gave matinées every afternoon of the week, and concerts and hops every evening, excepting Sunday, when the program was somewhat changed, and a so-called sacred concert was given, and always embodied music of a high order.

One evening, Helen and Marjorie met face to face at one of the hops.

It was strange that they had not encountered each

other before, for both were in the habit of frequenting the place, but they had happened to go on different nights, and so they had never met until now.

Both had been waltzing, and had passed each other on the same floor several times, but Marjorie's eyes were always downcast, even though her dress often touched Helen's as they whirled by each other, and thus the latter had no opportunity to recognize her.

After one of the dances, Dr. Black conducted his fiancée to the veranda, which ran around three sides of the building, and was always brilliantly lighted, seated her at one of the tables there, and then left her to order some ices.

Here Helen, who was promenading the piazza on the arm of the gentleman with whom she had been dancing, came suddenly upon her.

She was lovely, in a dainty white India mull, made over rose-colored silk, and wore a broad-brimmed Leghorn hat, trimmed with white plumes and a dash of rose color under the brim. She did not look a day older than when Marjorie had bidden her farewell, two years ago, in the Adirondacks, although there was an unwonted look of sadness in her eyes.

Marjorie's heart bounded into her throat as she saw her approaching, and she involuntarily started to her feet just as she came opposite her.

"Helen!" her lips framed the word, but no sound issued from them, and she would have been glad if the floor had opened at that moment and swallowed her from sight.

Helen excused herself to her companion, and drew nearer to her, with extended hand and a smile on her lips.

"Marjorie," she said in the old, sweet, friendly tones, "I have long known that you were in the city, but we have never happened to meet before. I am glad to see you, dear."

CHAPTER XII.

AN UNEXPECTED HONOR.

AND she was glad to see her.

If Mrs. Ellsworth had done her mother an irreparable injury in the past, and was still determined to persecute her, Marjorie could not be held responsible for the wrongdoing of her mother, and so Helen had never treasured any ill feeling against her on account of it.

She had never had any reason to suspect the girl of having done her a wilful injury. She knew that she had learned to love Rob, and she had believed that she had won him from her; but, supposing that had come around only in a natural way, from their constant companionship, she had told herself that was no reason why she should withdraw her friendship from the girl. She had never confided to Marjorie that Rob was more to her than the "school friend" which she had represented him, and she did not dream that she had fathomed her secret, and yet had deliberately set herself to win him away from her. After her confession of love for him, there had seemed to come a barrier between them, and their correspondence had fallen off; nevertheless, she had continued to be fond of her, not even allowing a spirit of jealousy to creep into her consciousness and sour her. Rob, she thought, was the recreant, not Marjorie.

She had wondered, after learning that Mrs. Ellsworth and her daughter were in Colorado Springs, and reduced to the necessity of keeping a boarding-house, where they had left Mrs. Sturdyvant and the rest of the party with whom they were traveling. If Marjorie had been engaged to Bob, where now was the young man, that he did not rescue his fiancée from the disagreeable life she was now leading?

Perhaps, however, she reasoned with scornfully curling lips, Mr. Lancaster, who had once been so fond of the girl, and who had been her ideal of an "old-time knight," had interfered when misfortune overtook her—as was evidently the case—and had refused to allow his nephew to marry out of the charmed sphere in which he moved.

Thus, out of the sweetness of her pure and loving nature, she tried to excuse, and think well of the friend in whom she had so implicitly trusted two years previous; thus, when she met her at the casino, and put out her hand to greet her, and observed, "I am glad to see you," she meant every word of it, and her earnest face corroborated her statement.

"Are you, really, Helen?" Marjorie questioned eagerly, while she searched the lovely eyes, looking so kindly into hers, though she blushed crimson from mingled gilt and shame. "I—I was afraid you would never speak to me again, especially after—after we came here, and—what has been said. I wanted to come to see you, but M—I—I could not," she faltered in conclusion, while her eyes drooped beneath the clear, steadfast look which Helen bent upon her.

"I understand you, Marjorie," our gentle heroine gravely returned; "and, of course, I could not expect you to come, under the circumstances. Nevertheless, if the conditions had been favorable, I should have been glad to have you do so, and I know of no reason why I should not want to speak to you; it certainly would not be kind or right to blame you for what others may have done. Mamma is here—inside the dance-hall; would you like to see her?" she queried, as she glanced beyond the glass partition that separated the veranda from the brilliantly lighted room.

"Oh, yes—but, perhaps, she would not care to meet me," said Marjorie, with evident embarassment.

"Mamma is not vindictive," responded Helen, with a friendly smile, "and she certainly would not impute to you what you are in no way responsible for."

"She is very good," said the girl, but with evident shrinking.

Then, glancing down the veranda, she saw Dr. Black approaching, and followed by a waiter, who was bearing a tray.

She heaved a sigh of relief at the prospect of having the uncomfortable—at least, to her—interview interrupted.

"Ah!" she said hurriedly, "I see my friend returning, and I shall have to wait until later." Then she added, with something of her old-time frankness and confiding manner: "But it was lovely of you, Helen, to come to speak to me. Give my love to Mrs. Seymour, and I hope we shall meet again soon."

She turned back to the table where she had been sitting, the doctor rejoining her at that moment, while Helen went back to her companion, but with a shadow of disappointment and perplexity resting on her fair face.

Later, when talking the incident over with her mother, Mrs. Seymour did not express herself either for or against Marjorie. She did not like to influence Helen against any one, but she had been impressed, at the time she had broken with Rob, that the girl was not true—she had not quite liked the tone of her letters, and now, under existing circumstances, she preferred that the two should not renew their friendship, although she did not say so.

She knew that Mrs. Ellsworth must still be working against her, for she was continually encountering people with whom she had been upon very friendly terms, during her sojourn with Mrs. Allen, who now were decidedly frigid in their greetings when they met, if, indeed, they saw her at all.

They continued to go to the casino, for they thoroughly enjoyed the fine music, and Helen loved to dance; but they never encountered Marjorie there again.

The summer flitted swiftly by, until August came in, when everybody began to manifest enthusiasm in view of the approaching Flower Carnival.

A whole week was usually devoted to the festivities, and nothing else was talked of for a whole month preceding; but the two most important events of the carnival were the society circus and flower days, the latter taking the precedence of all else. Ladies, young and old, spared no time, labor, or expense in perfecting their designs for carriages and costumes, many of them making thousands of paper flowers with which to decorate their traps. Gentlemen arranged their various committees, and talked of horses, vehicles, and liveries; the prizes to be awarded, colors of the banners, route of procession, et cetera, et cetera. In fact, the entire city was given up generally to preparations for the long-looked-for event.

One morning, during the first week of August, a couple of cards were handed into Mrs. Seymour's room, where she and Helen were having a quiet chat over their sewing.

"For Mrs. and Miss Seymour," said the servant who presented them; "and the lady is waiting in the parlor."

"Why, mamma, it is Miss Wallace!" Helen exclaimed, flushing slightly, as she glanced at the inscription upon the bits of pasteboard.

Mrs. Seymour glanced up from her work in surprise,

the color deepening upon her own cheeks, and a spark of fire in her usually mild eyes.

"What can she want, after all these weeks, I wonder?" she observed in a constrained tone.

The Wallaces were a wealthy and influential family, who had long resided in the city, and were regarded as one of the "first families" in the place.

Mr. Wallace had been a United States senator some years previous, then had spent a long time in Europe, traveling, and educating some of his children, after which he had come to Colorado Springs, and erected a palatial residence on Cascade Avenue, with the intention of making the city a permanent home.

He had a very interesting family, consisting of one son and three daughters, Miss Hetty Wallace being the eldest of these. The family had met Mrs. Seymour and her daughter at a church reception during the winter, and had been charmed with them. Calls were exchanged, then an intimacy between Helen and Miss Hetty had sprung up, and for a long time the most friendly relations had existed between the two families, Mrs. Wallace often sending her carriage for Mrs. Seymour to either drive or spend the day with her.

But of late they had seen nothing of any of them, and Mrs. Seymour, being extremely sensitive, had, naturally, inferred that the Wallaces must have heard the reports that had been so persistently circulated, and, like others, had seen fit to drop their acquaintance; hence this call from Miss Wallace was a genuine surprise.

"Of course, we must go down, mamma," said Helen, who had not failed to observe her mother's constraint.

"Yes, I suppose we must," she replied, as she laid aside her work, and arose with some reluctance, and the two went down together.

The moment they appeared in sight, however, there

was the sound of a glad little cry, the rush of silken
skirts, as a tall, slim, lovely girl flew to Helen's side,
encircled her in her arms, and gave her a hearty kiss.

"What an age it seems since I saw you last!" she
said breezily; "and, dear Mrs. Seymour, how well you
are looking! I suppose you received my note, telling
you of our sudden flitting?" she added, turning again
to Helen, who had been somewhat taken aback by her
effusive greeting.

"No, I have heard nothing from you," she replied.

"Why, how strange!" cried the girl, flushing to her
brows. "I dashed off a few lines to you, and sent it
by the coachman, the morning we went away. Why,
you surely must have felt as if you had been uncere-
moniously deserted!" she concluded in a remorseful
tone.

"Ah, then you have been away?" smilingly returned
Mrs. Seymour, as she cordially clasped the hand extended to her, for the burden of doubt all rolled from
her heart at Miss Wallace's unmistakable friendliness.

"Yes. Mamma was suddenly sent for, to go to
Glenwood Springs, to her favorite sister, who had
been sent there for her health, and was taken very
much worse after being there for a week or two. As
it was evident she would have to remain with her for
some time, papa said he would take us girls to Salt
Lake, and some other places that we have long been
wanting to visit. Tom went East to spend the month
of July with a friend, and we have had a most delightful six weeks' trip, although we did not dream
of being gone half that time; but mamma could not
leave her sister, and papa said we might as well make
the most of her enforced absence. We only returned
last evening, and I came right away this morning to
see how you are. I cannot understand, though, why
Dave should have neglected to deliver my note. I
shall take him to task as soon as I go home."

"Never mind, dear; it is all right now that we know about it; but we had wondered a little what had become of you all," Mrs. Seymour kindly returned. "I trust your mother's sister has recovered."

Miss Hetty shot a quick glance at her, and flushed again.

"Yes, Aunt Mattie is well again, though, for awhile, her life was despaired of," she replied. "Mamma sent her love to you, and is coming to take you for a drive this afternoon, if you have no other engagement."

Mrs. Seymour thanked her, with shining eyes, and said she should be very happy to accept the invitation.

She was greatly cheered by the girl's explanations regarding what had seemed like studied neglect, and also by the evidence of the continued friendship of the family.

"And now for my errand," continued Miss Hetty, with sparkling eyes, "for I have a very important one—guess it, you brown-eyed beauty!" she interposed, as she gave Helen an impulsive little hug.

"I am sure I haven't the slightest suspicion of its nature," Helen returned, with a bright laugh, for she also was very happy to have her friend back again.

"Well, then, I will not keep you in suspense," pursued Miss Hetty. "Papa has consented to allow me to drive a trap in the Flower Carnival this year, and, of course, I am all on the qui vive over it. I want it to be very, very swell, you know. I am to have the span of blacks, and carte ' lanche, and, knowing what exquisite taste you have, Mrs. Seymour, 1 have ventured to come to ask if you will kindly help me design the decorations for the trap?"

"I shall be delighted to do so, Miss Hetty," said Mrs. Seymour, with animation; "it will give me great pleasure. Have you anything in mind as yet?"

"I haven't an idea," said the girl helplessly; "and papa insists that I must not, on any account, annoy

mamma—she has so many other cares just now—so"
—with a sly glance at Helen—"I have audaciously
come to bother somebody else's mamma."

"I have nothing else to do, and I should enjoy it
immensely," said Mrs. Seymour eagerly, adding:
"Only, you must give me a day or two to think about
it before I propose any design."

"Oh, certainly; take more time, if you wish, for we
have nearly three weeks before us, you know. I mention it now because I felt that I must set the ball rolling. And, now, I have another favor to ask," she
went on, the color flushing her cheeks again; "would
you object to have Helen ride with me in the procession? I should feel awfully stiff and forlorn to go
alone in the trap, with the eyes of all those thousands
upon me."

Mrs. Seymour had been quick to note the flush, and
she felt a lump swelling in her throat at this proposal.

She knew, as well as if she had been told, that there
was a double purpose in the invitation.

There had not been the slightest hint that the Wallaces knew aught of the invidious reports that had
been circulated, but she felt impressed that they had
reached their ears, and that they had taken this way
—which was true—to show to them, and to the whole
city, their loyalty to them, and their contempt for
the miserable scandal. It certainly was a beautiful
and delicate way of proving their friendship, and Mrs.
Seymour was quick to appreciate it.

"Indeed, no; I could not have the slightest objection—if Helen herself would like it," she said, turning
to her, with a smile that had a suspicion of tears in it.

"Ah, Helen, say yes; there's a dear," pleaded Miss
Wallace eagerly. "I have set my heart upon having
you go with me."

"Of course I shall like it; I think it will be great

fun, only you must allow me also to help you get ready for the great event," Helen responded, with a very bright face.

"Thank you, but I intended to draft you into the service, as well as your mother," said Hetty, laughing. "Then, you know, I shall have to drive the blacks every day between now and then, to get used to them, and have them get used to me, and I shall want you to ride with me. Of course, the coachman will go with us, to drill me in handling the ribbons, and give me points in general, so there will be no fear of our getting into any trouble."

And Helen, seeing a great deal of enjoyment before her, cordially assented to her proposition.

Then they all fell to chatting of things in general, in the most friendly and social way, until the clock on the mantel struck twelve, when Miss Hetty, with a cry of dismay at having stayed so long, arose to go.

"My dear," said Mrs. Seymour, when she and Helen were again in their own room, after the departure of their guest, "nothing could be more lovely of the Wallaces, or have been more delicately planned and suggested; I had wronged them in my thought, believing, since we neither saw nor heard anything of them, that they had fallen away from us, like so many others. But it is evident that they believe in us, and intend to do everything in their power to make it apparent. Mrs. Wallace will take me out this afternoon—you will ride with Miss Hetty every day until the carnival, and I imagine that public opinion will eventually veer around in our favor."

Helen turned, and laid her arms around her mother's neck, and there were tears in her beautiful eyes.

"I am very, very glad, for your sake, mamma, dear," she said tremulously, "for it has broken my heart to have you so cruelly traduced. Why is it that the world is so ungenerous? Why are people so eager to

believe the worst of others—roll gossip, like a sweet
morsel, under their tongues, and ignore that which is
good, and noble, and pure in characters like yours?"

"It does seem unaccountable," Mrs. Seymour
gravely responded; "but it is a habit that is very
easily acquired, and that is why I would never allow
you to repeat things that you heard against your
mates at school; if you had that which was pleasant
and praiseworthy to say of any one, I was always
ready to hear it, as you know."

"Yes; and I can now see how wise you were," said
Helen. Then she went on thoughtfully: "What possible good can it do any one to carry malicious reports from one to another? And what advantage
does any one gain by giving people, of whom they
hear something evil, the cold shoulder? They hear
only one side of the story—they take no pains to ascertain whether it is true or false, and yet they form
their opinions, and judge the victim from the disparaging rumors."

"I know, dear, that seems to have been our experience this summer, but it is a long lane that has no
turning, you know, and, as we are beginning to find
out," replied Mrs. Seymour, smiling, "there are some
just and high-minded people in the world, and it is a
comfort to know that you can number some of them
among your friends. It is a great pity that those
who love gossip cannot realize that they only demoralize themselves by trading in it, and that they
by no means establish their own virtue and morality
by trying to trample others down, and assuming a
'holier than thou' attitude toward them."

CHAPTER XIII.

IN GREEN AND WHITE.

THE following two or three weeks were very busy ones with our friends, but they were also very enjoyable.

Mrs. Seymour, with her genius for designing, and her exquisite taste, presented Miss Wallace, after a few days of thought, with an artistic conception for her trap which delighted that young lady's heart, and won highest encomiums from her friends; and then, as they could not do anything about the decorations —which were to comprise only natural flowers—until two or three days before the carnival, they turned their attention to the all-important costumes for the two young ladies, and which were also to be supervised by Mrs. Seymour.

There was, of course, much running back and forth, to say nothing of the excitement of shopping, and the studying of fashion-plates.

The Seymours were often at the Wallaces, where two dainty dresses were in process of construction, and thus, with the driving every day, to coach the fair aspirant for carnival honors, Helen always accompanying her; with Mrs. Seymour's frequent appearance in Mrs. Wallace's handsome victoria, there began to appear upon many faces whom they met looks of wonder and perplexity, not to mention curious comments regarding the meaning of it all.

Our busy spinster was especially exercised on account of it. "I just don't understand it," she observed, with considerable asperity, to a knot of her fellow-boarders, who were discussing the matter. "Why, the Wallaces are on the topmost wave here. I really think that Mrs. Wallace ought to be informed of the truth, and warned that her daughter will be seriously compromised if she continues to go about so with that Seymour girl; everybody is commenting upon the intimacy."

A few days later, she met Mrs. Wallace in one of the stores down-town, at the ribbon counter, where that lady was purchasing numerous bolts of wide white satin ribbon.

"Ah!" blandly observed Miss Lampson. "I perceive that you are preparing for the carnival! I saw by this morning's paper that Miss Wallace is entered for the procession."

"Yes; Hetty was anxious to participate last year, but her father, who had then but just purchased the horses she wished to drive, did not think it would be safe to gratify her. This year, however, he felt that it would be all right to grant her desire," Mrs. Wallace explained.

"I expect she will come out with something pretty fine," said the spinster curiously.

"Well," returned her companion, smiling—for she well knew the woman's propensity—"we are going to let her do pretty much as she wants to, and, as some friends are kindly assisting her, I hope she will be satisfied with the results."

"Oh-o! was Miss Lampson's mental ejaculation, as light began to dawn upon her. "I'll bet the Seymours are helping her get up the rig. Well, a dressmaker is supposed to know how to make pretty bows and knots," but a contemptuous sniff was the only outward sign of these cogitations. Then, aloud, she remarked:

"I see Helen Seymour riding with Miss Wallace a great deal—they appear to be exceedingly friendly."

"Yes; we are all very fond of Helen, as well as of her mother," replied Mrs. Wallace, with a slight uplifting of her proud head.

"Are you?" queried the spinster, with significant emphasis. "Really, I feel sorry to hear you say so, for—of course, I do not mean to be officious, Mrs. Wallace, and I have all the charity and sympathy in the world for those unfortunate ladies—for I wonder if you know what the whole city has been saying about them during the last three or four months! It —it would be a great pity to have Miss Wallace compromised."

"I beg your pardon, Miss Lampson," Mrs. Wallace here interposed, and she looked very tall, and straight, and imposing, as she said it, "but my daughter can never be compromised by her association with Miss Seymour, who is one of the loveliest girls I have ever known, and her mother is a rare, sweet woman. Yes, I have known what the 'whole city'—though I think that is rather a sweeping statement—have been saying about these people, whom I am proud to claim as friends, and I am free to declare that I am almost ashamed to be numbered among such a gossiping and uncharitable community. Ah, here comes my package. Good morning, Miss Lampson!"

And the lady of "the topmost wave" sailed away, with a superior air, leaving her recent companion in a decidedly wilted condition.

"Humph! She carried it off with a high head; but I reckon they will find out, to their sorrow, that they cannot show contempt for public opinion to any such extent with impunity," she muttered, with a very red face.

And this poor, poverty-stricken woman—poverty-stricken from a moral point of view, although she possessed an abundance of this world's goods—went her way, with her fresh morsels to regale the itching ears of her associates in a gossiping boarding-house.

Marien Ellsworth's jealousy was newly aroused upon learning of the Seymours' intimacy with the Wallaces, and she became more bitter than ever in her insinuations and malicious thrusts.

So "Carnival Week" drew on apace, and on Monday morning preceding "Flower Day," which had been set for Wednesday, the party from abroad arrived in Colorado Springs.

Mrs. Sturdyvant went directly to Mrs. Ellsworth, but the others of the company repaired to "The Antlers," where they had rooms engaged, having telegraphed ahead for them some weeks previous.

The whole week, as previously stated, was given up to festivity. On Monday evening, the carnival was formally opened by a grand ball at the casino, at Broadmore, and was said to be the most brilliant affair of the kind in the history of the city.

Tuesday was devoted to the great carnival circus, which was said to be the "funniest thing that ever happened," as the parade was "a burlesque from start to finish," and originated with, and was carried out by, the society young men of the city. It was well done in every detail, and was a huge success.

Then came Wednesday, as fair a day as ever broke or gladdened expectant hearts in this land of perpetual sunshine, and which was regarded as the most important day of the festival.

Two huge grand stands had been erected—one on either side of Cascade Avenue, not far from "The Antlers"—and these were covered by an immense canvas, to protect the people from the blazing sun. Midway of these was the judges' stand, behind which was located the band, which discoursed inspiriting music, and by two o'clock every seat was occupied, while many hundreds of people stood outside and along the route of the parade.

Mr. Lancaster and Rob, with the other members of their party from "The Antlers," had taken one of the boxes, a tier of which had been arranged on both sides of the grand stand, and raised only a little above the avenue through which the procession was to pass.

As it happened, it was directly opposite the governor's box, and about midway of the stand, and thus it commanded a fine view of everything, while, too, their conspicuous position made it easy to single them out.

Both gentlemen were looking unusually well, and appeared to be in good spirits.

It had been a great relief to them—though neither had given expression to it—when Mrs. Ellsworth and Marjorie left the party, and throughout the remainder of their trip, they had experienced a sense of freedom which neither had enjoyed previous to their departure.

Mr. Lancaster was, at times, oppressed by a feeling of obligation to Mrs. Ellsworth, and this was increased after learning from Mrs. Sturdyvant of the ill tidings that had greeted her upon her arrival at Colorado Springs, and which had necessitated her remaining there, and opening a boarding-house, to supply her daily needs.

Upon hearing what exorbitant rent she was obliged to pay for her house, he had conceived the prospect of purchasing and presenting her with a house, when he should arrive upon the scene, and in this scheme—upon being consulted—Rob most heartily concurred.

A little incident, showing how small the world really is, and which also has its bearing upon other points in our story, occurred soon after our travelers had taken their seats in the grand stand.

In the box adjoining theirs, there sat a richly dressed woman, whose face instantly attracted Mr. Lancaster, although she evidently had not as yet observed him.

"She looks, for all the world, as if she might be Althea Lampson, of thirty years ago, even though she has grown stout, and old, and gray," he said to himself, as he covertly watched her out of the corner of his eye.

He could have reached out his hand and touched her, and yet she was wholly unconscious that a ghost from out her past was in such close proximity to her, for she was absorbed in watching the people who were passing and repassing, and the notables who were occupying the boxes on the opposite stand, and commenting upon them to her companions.

Mr. Lancaster could easily overhear what she was saying, and a smile of amusement curled his fine lips from time to time.

"She is Althea, sure enough," he said, "and, if I am not mistaken, she is still just as deeply interested in the affairs of her neighbors as she used to be in the old days. I wonder how she happens to be way out here, and what has become of—— Well, I'm afraid I am getting curious myself," he concluded, cutting short his soliloquy, with a shrug of his broad shoulders.

They had to wait a long time for the parade, for the time set for it to start was two-thirty, while it was to form upon the college reservation, more than a mile from the stand; meantime, however, the band "did itself proud" for the entertainment of the waiting thousands.

During one of the pauses, while the musicians were taking a rest, Mr. Lancaster leaned forward, and, with a courteous bow, observed:

"I beg pardon, but am I not addressing Miss Lampson, formerly of Richmond, Virginia?"

The woman looked around suddenly at the question, and her lips contracted spasmodically, as she lifted a startled, wondering glance to the gentleman.

"Yes," she faltered reluctantly. Then, after studying his face intently for a moment, she exclaimed: "Why, can it be possible? Yes, I am sure you are Halburton Lancaster!" and she extended her hand to him, although not without manifest constraint in her manner.

"You are right," Mr. Lancaster smilingly returned; "but I little thought that I should meet any one whom I had known in my youth, away out here among the mines and mountains of Colorado. But, surely, you are not out here for your health, Miss Lampson?" he concluded, as his eye rested inquiringly upon her ruddy face and portly figure.

"Oh, no; I am in perfect health, but I—I like the climate here," she responded, flushing, and her glance wavering beneath his. "I have been here for a good many years, with now and then a trip to New York, Boston, and San Francisco, to vary the monotony."

"It truly is a delightful place, although I have not seen very much of it as yet, though I have had interests here for some time. It is a wonderful country, and I would not mind remaining here myself for a few years," her companion appreciatively responded.

"Then this your first visit to Colorado? When did you arrive?" Miss Lampson inquired, while her keen eyes were quick to observe the richness of his attire, the rare white stone upon his shirt-front, and his distinguished appearance in general.

"On Monday morning. My nephew"—with a glance at Rob—"and I have been traveling abroad for a couple of years; in fact, have made a tour of the world, and are now on our way home."

"Your nephew!" repeated the spinster, while she shot a curious glance at the young man. "I imagined

he might be your son—I saw you when you came in
together, but did not once dream you were any one
whom I had ever known."

"No; I have no son," replied the gentleman, with
an involuntary sigh. "I am alone in the world but for
Rob."

"Ah! Is that so?" observed the woman in a tone of
surprise. She seemed about to add something more,
but at that instant the strains of another band were
borne to them from up the avenue, and she exclaimed,
instead:

"Ah, the procession is coming at last! But"—as a
fierce gust of wind swept through the place, bringing
a heavy cloud of dust with it—"I'm awfully afraid
we're going to have a sand-storm! How annoying!"

Every eye was now turned expectantly up the
avenue, and, presently, the long-looked-for parade
came into view, headed by the chief marshal, mounted
on a fine charger. He was followed by a platoon of
police, in parade dress. Then came Company A of
"National Reserves;" after them, novelties in bicycles
—unique designs of every description. Then the "cowboy division," followed by a band of Indians, chiefs,
squaws, and children. After them came the children's
division, and a beautiful sight it was! A tiny sprite,
in white, seated in a huge shell, composed of gorgeous
pink roses, and drawn by two plump white ponies that
were led by a couple of pages in white and silver, attracted the delighted applause of the multitude, as
did also many other designs. Following the juveniles,
the flower parade proper came into view, and this
comprised vehicles of every description, decorated in
the most gorgeous and beautiful manner, with flowers
of innumerable varieties, both natural and artificial.

It would be impossible to give a detailed description
of the magnificent display, which occupied a long time
in passing the grand stand, all aspirants receiving

their share of praise and appreciation, and showers of flowers strewn in their pathway. About half of the procession had entered and passed the grand stand, when the spectators went suddenly wild with enthusiasm, which clearly evinced that something more than ordinarily attractive had come into sight. This was caused by the appearance of an equipage which certainly would have been a dream of beauty for the brush of an artist.

The trap was a one-seated affair, very natty and stylish in shape. It was completely covered—not a particle of woodwork being visible—with immense natural white chrysanthemums, among which quantities of delicate, feathery asparagus-vine had been entwined, and which contributed an airy effect to the tout ensemble that was indescribably beautiful. The spokes of the wheels had been wound with white satin ribbon; a row of perfect chrysanthemums encircled the rims, while around the hubs the same flowers had been massed to form a huge star, and over all the feathery veil of green. On the back and the dasher, which were also a mass of white, a great letter W had been wrought in solid green. On each corner of the trap, and on either side of the seat, there was a huge bouquet of the same exquisite blossoms, tied with broad white satin ribbons. The thills also had been covered with ribbon.

The horses, splendid specimens, were black as Erebus, and having been groomed until they shone like satin, were handsome enough of themselves to have taken a prize. Their harness had been covered with white, also the lines. They wore collars of chrysanthemums, and one huge snowy blossom just back of each ear.

The floor and seat of the trap were a mass of asparagus-vine, and upon this emerald throne there were seated two beautiful girls, clad in elegant costumes of spotless white—all save their hats, which were of dead black, with great, graceful, nodding black plumes, just the color of the horses.

These young ladies were Miss Hetty Wallace and Helen Seymour, and the former handled the ribbons, to guide her prancing steeds, with a grace and skill that drew forth round after round of applause, and an avalanche of blossoms from the delighted beholders, and which plainly indicated that, of all the vehicles which had as yet appeared, this symphony in green and white had won the palm.

As it drew near the box where Rob was sitting, he touched his uncle on the arm, and exclaimed:

"Look! This is the finest thing I have seen yet! Ah——"

His glance had first rested upon the magnificent horses, then swept on the beautiful trap, its chaste and unique decorations arousing his enthusiastic admiration. Next, he had noted the handsome and self-possessed girl who held the lines, with such an air of assurance in her white-gloved hands, and then— his eyes rested upon Helen, just as he spoke to Mr. Lancaster.

He recognized her instantly, and the shock that quivered through him, nearly depriving him of his senses, wrenched that agonized exclamation from him, and deprived him of his color, leaving him almost as white as the flowers among which the girl whom he adored sat embowered.

Mr. Lancaster also saw and recognized her, and was scarcely less moved than his nephew, while he was amazed, in view of the strange coincidence which had ordained that she should be in Colorado Springs at the same time with themselves.

Helen, fortunately for her self-possession, had not seen either of the gentlemen amid the sea of faces around her, and the trap passed on.

The parade, after passing the grand stand, moved on past "The Antlers" to another street, where it turned and countermarched, then passed through the grand stand again, each vehicle pausing before the judges to receive their verdict and awards.

It is needless to say that both Rob and Mr. Lancaster watched most eagerly for the reappearance of the symphony in green and white.

It came into view at last, the faces of the two girls within it all aglow with delight, in view of the enthusiasm which their turnout had aroused.

When they paused before the judges, a white satin banner, bearing upon it, in golden letters, the words, "First Prize," was passed up to Helen, who received it with smiling thanks, and amid deafening applause.

But, as the trap moved on, and the fair girl glanced right and left, as if in serach of some one, her eyes suddenly fell upon Rob, who was leaning forward, and gazing at her, with all his heart in his own.

Their glances met, and held each other for one brief moment; then she was gone, and without a sign of recognition on the part of either.

CHAPTER XIV.

MISS LAMPSON BECOMES COMMUNICATIVE.

"OH, Helen, wasn't it just delightful! And isn't it lovely that we have taken the first prize in our class? But we owe it all to your mother, dearie, and I am going to have one of the photographs that we had taken of the trap just before we started out copied in crayon, and enlarged for her. Do you think it will please her? But, Helen! What is it? You look like a ghost! Are you ill?"

Miss Wallace had been so elated upon receiving the first prize that, on leaving the grand stand, she burst forth as above, and chattered on like a magpie, not once looking at her friend until she had guided her horses out into the open avenue, and somewhat away from the crowd; and then, as Helen had made no reply to her, she turned to her, and was astonished and dismayed to find her lying limply back in her seat, and as pale as the blossoms around her.

"I—I think I am a trifle faint," Helen murmured weakly. Then, as she saw the anxious look in Hetty's eyes, she tried to smile, and added: "But I shall soon be all right again."

"Has the excitement been too much for you?" pursued Miss Wallace. "Were you frightened at the horses when they pranced so before the judges' stand?"

"No, I was not at all frightened. I was proud of them, they looked so handsome. And you managed them beautifully, Hetty. I was proud of you, too, and I am delighted that you took the first prize," Helen returned, making a mighty effort to recover her self-possession and her strength, which had entirely deserted her when she found herself so unexpectedly gazing into the yearning eyes of the man whom she loved with all her heart and soul.

"Ah! Now you are beginning to look a little more like yourself," said Miss Hetty, who had been watching her anxiously. "I really was afraid that you were going to faint away—there was no more color in your face than in your dress. What caused it, dear?" she persisted.

"I—I think—yes, I am quite sure, it must have been the excitement of—of everything," she replied. Then, glancing up at the banner, to draw her friend's attention from herself, for she was trembling in every nerve, with the knowledge that Rob was in the city—she said: "It is a lovely banner, Hetty; it is a great honor to have won it, and I feel very grand to be carrying it."

"Yes; I was almost wild with delight when I saw them handing it to you," said the girl, regarding her trophy with a fond look. "And how everybody cheered and applauded! Ah, my black beauties"—with an approving nod at her handsome steeds—"you look as if you were in bridal attire, and I think it very becoming of you. It really was the prettiest trap in the parade, and I know that papa will be just as proud as we are. Now, would you like to drive around town a little before we go home? Our pretty rig will be all faded by to-morrow, and I am sure there are some sick people on the south side, who could not get out to-day, who would be glad to get a glimpse of some of the glory of the carnival."

Yes, Helen said, she would like to ride for awhile, and so they turned toward the poorer quarter of the city, to allow hungry eyes to feast upon their dainty turnout.

When the Wallace equipage had passed before the judges' stand, and the first prize had been passed up to Helen, Miss Lampson tossed her head angrily, and gave vent to a spiteful sneer, for she had not yet recovered from the rebuff which she had received from Mrs. Wallace a few days previous.

"Well, it's a pretty enough trap, I'll admit that," she remarked to a lady beside her, but in a tone loud enough for Mr. Lancaster—who was also in a decidedly uncomfortable frame of mind—to catch every word; "but I, for one, can't uphold anybody in defying public opinion to such an extent."

"Yes, the trap was beautiful, and they were really the prettiest and most effectively gotten up girls in the procession," observed her companion.

"They're pretty enough; I haven't a word to say against their looks, and the rig really deserved the first prize in their class, in my opinion. If Miss Wallace had driven alone, it would have been all right; but, to have that Seymour girl flaunting that white satin banner in all our faces, after all that has been said, goes decidedly against the grain with me," Miss Lampson rejoined in a malignant tone, and evidently in a very uncomfortable frame of mind.

Mr. Lancaster had given a violent start when she had spoken Helen's name, and a hot flush dyed his face crimson for a moment.

"I beg your pardon," he said, leaning toward her, during the pause that followed her last remark, "but can you tell me the names of the young ladies who rode in that green and white trap with the black horses?"

"Yes," replied Miss Lampson; "the one who drove is Miss Hetty Wallace, the eldest daughter of Honorable R. S. Wallace, of this city. The girl who rode with her is Miss Helen Seymour, from New York."

"Miss Helen Seymour?" repeated Mr. Lancaster, with paling lips and a tremendous heart-throb.

"Yes; she and her mother have been here for nearly a year. Mrs. Seymour was very feeble when she came, and hardly any one thought she would ever be any better; but she is perfectly well now. She used to be a dressmaker in New York City," explained the voluble spinster, with a slighting inflection as she mentioned the woman's trade.

But Mr. Lancaster thought nothing of it just then. He was amazed to learn that Helen was still Miss Seymour, and, such being the fact, he realized at once that her marriage with Hubert Alton must have been interrupted.

"What could it mean?" he questioned, within himself, and with a whirling brain.

He had never heard anything more from Hubert after receiving his telegram announcing the date of his marriage; but he had not thought strange of that.

The next time he heard from Mr. Rice, his business manager, that gentleman wrote that his instructions regarding the sum to be deposited to Alton's account had been carried out. This letter had been written on the very day that Hubert was supposed to have been married, Mr. Rice mentioning the fact that the groom-elect was away, having been given the day because of the important event.

The next news from the firm told him that the manager had died very suddenly, the following week, but his place had been immediately filled by his son, who also had served him for many years.

Mr. Lancaster had, of course, been saddened by the loss, but, as the business was prospering, and he knew that the Junior Rice was competent to fill his father's position, he did not concern himself regarding details. Thus, no reference ever afterward having been made to Alton, or the sum that had been deposited to his

account, he had, naturally, supposed that the young
man had drawn his money long ago, and the transaction would appear upon the books when he came to
examine them upon his return; and so he had given
no further thought to that matter.

But, evidently, no marriage had ever taken place.
It was passing strange, since he had had word from
Alton only a few days previous to the date set for
it, that Helen was to become his wife on a certain
day, at noon.

Then came another startling thought.

"If Rob learns the truth, he will never rest until he
and the girl are reunited. I don't care," he mentally
added, a great burden rolling off his heart, and with
a feeling of freedom, such as he had not experienced
in two years; "he shall have his own way about it,
and God bless them both. She is certainly lovely
enough to turn almost anybody's head. He has suffered enough through my sin, and I am only too
thankful to learn that I am not quite so guilty as I
have seemed."

He glanced askance at Rob.

The young man, evidently, had heard nothing of
what Miss Lampson had said about Helen, and he
was sitting grave and preoccupied, and with a look
of pain in his handsome eyes that cut his uncle to the
heart.

"You say the Seymours came from New York?" he
observed to Miss Lampson, for the sake of learning
more about the girl, for he saw that she was well
posted regarding both mother and daughter.

"Yes; they boarded in the same house with me for
several months, until—well, you'll hear it from some
one else, if I don't tell it—until a scandal arose, and
that had to go elsewhere. Mrs. Seymour is with the
Wallaces to-day—in the third box to the left of the
governor—you will see her as soon as this victoria

passes," and Miss Lampson craned her own neck, to get a better view of the woman who had excited her bitterest jealousy.

The victoria passed, and Mr. Lancaster's glance sought the third box on the left of the governor.

Then he sat suddenly erect, a startled look in his eyes.

"Which one of the ladies is she?" he queried almost sharply.

"The one in the light-gray tailor-made suit. She has on a black lace hat, with pink trimmings."

Miss Lampson was herself so interested in studying the effective costume she had described—for Mrs. Seymour was always artistically and stylishly arrayed—that she did not observe anything peculiar about her questioner, who sat as if he had been suddenly turned to stone, a look of mingled agony and wonder frozen on his colorless face.

His hands were clenched so tightly that, for days afterward, he bore the print of his nails upon his palm, while his lips were compressed into a livid hue.

"She is a very handsome woman," the spinster rambled on, and, although her voice sounded afar off, and he did not appear to hear her, he heard every word, which, later, stung him to the soul with its malice and poison. "She dresses like a queen, and her taste is simply exquisite. She is mighty high-toned, too, in spite of a scandalous mystery that enshrouds her history. Why, they say that neither she nor her daughter has a right to the name they bear—though they claim that the girl's father died before she was born—and even worse things. But how the wind does blow! It is getting to be a perfect gale. Look! Heavens! I believe the stand is giving away over there!" she concluded, starting from her seat in alarm.

There seemed to be a good reason for her fears, for

the wind, which had been increasing in violence, was now rising almost to a tempest, and, sweeping in under the canvas that covered the grand stand, filled it like a balloon, wrenching and straining it in a frightful manner until the timbers which supported it began to sway and crack ominously, and the people on the upper seats were hastily vacating them, and hurrying from the place.

Those in the boxes, however, did not at first appear to be alarmed, the police along the avenue assuring them there was no danger, and advising them to keep their seats, as the end of the parade was now in sight.

But all at once, a stronger gust than any that had preceded it, stretched the canvas aloft with such force that the wooden supports on one end of the stand snapped like pipe-stems, and then sent it swooping down upon the seats below.

This was on the side where the governor was sitting, and now there began a general stampede.

The sight and the danger served to unlock Halburton Lancaster's paralyzed senses.

He had not once taken his eyes from that beautiful woman in the box occupied by the Wallaces, and no one will ever know the agony the man endured during those few horrible moments, when it seemed to him that an avenging angel must have driven him there to have retributive justice meted out to him.

As the supports snapped, and came crashing down, the man sprang to his feet, with a groan.

"Margaret!" The name burst from his livid lips in a tone that bespoke almost mortal anguish, while a thousand heartrending thoughts went sweeping through his brain, searing it as with a hot iron.

Miss Lampson had fled, with her friends, and now, as the flapping canvas and creaking boards warned others to do likewise, Mr. Lancaster gave vent to a hoarse cry of despair.

"Margaret! My God! What have I done?" he almost sobbed.

Then, to Rob's astonishment, he leaped over the railing of their box, dashed across the avenue, barely escaping the wheels of the last team in the procession, and made his way among the hurrying crowd to that box opposite, where Mr. Wallace, with a white, anxious face, was trying to reassure his frightened family, and conduct them safely to the ground.

Mr. Lancaster at last reached the spot, and held out his hands to Mrs. Seymour, who had risen from her chair, and was looking around for the best way to help herself out of the place.

"Margaret! Come! Give me your hands, and I will help you safely over the railing! Trust me—I will save you!" were the pleading sentences that he flung desperately at her.

She turned her wondering eyes upon the man, as she heard him pronounce her name.

Then she, too, froze, and stood staring helplessly at him in blank and horrified amazement.

"Hal!" The name slipped from her lips in voiceless agony.

"Come" he reiterated, with an anxious look aloft, as another gust noisly flapped the heavy canvas.

But the woman drew herself erect, with a mighty effort, and shrank away from him.

"Never!" she breathed, but with hueless lips.

Then her strength suddenly failed her; she collapsed, and sank, fainting, back upon the chair from which she had arisen a few moments before.

Mr. Wallace had seen the stranger offering to assist his guest, and, with a feeling of intense relief—but without observing anything peculiar in the situa-

tion—had then given his attention entirely to his
wife and two daughters, whom he readily conducted
to a place of safety; for, after that last fierce gust,
the wind suddenly began to subside, and, as the remaining supports still held firm, people began to
realize that the danger was over, and, indeed, had
not been so great as had been feared.

Mr. Lancaster was quick to appreciate this, especially as the fire department, which had figured conspicuously in the parade, had flown to the rescue, and
were now propping the canvas up, and away from
the fleeing crowd.

He, therefore, deliberately set himself about reviving his unconscious companion, using a vinaigrette,
which she had with her, and which he instantly recognized as one which she used to carry years ago.

"Margaret! Margaret!" he whispered tenderly in
her ear; "wake up, dear—wake up, and let me take
you away."

He chafed her hands and temples with one hand,
while he supported her with his other arm, until
some one from below called out "Here!" and a glass
of water was passed up to him.

He grasped it eagerly, and, pouring some upon the
woman's dainty handkerchief, he bathed her face and
head.

A heavy sigh told him, ere long, that his efforts
were being rewarded, and, putting the glass to her
lips, he bade her drink, in a tone of gentle authority,
which caused her, instinctively, to obey him.

The icy draft revived her almost immediately, and,
presently, she sat up, and turned her wondering glance
upon her companion.

"Go! Leave me!" she murmured faintly, but with a
repelling gesture.

"No, I will not, Margaret," he replied in a low,
almost fierce, tone. "I have searched the world over

for you, and I will never leave you until I have set myself right with you; then, if you bid me go, unforgiven, I will never trouble you again. Come! I am going to take you to 'The Antlers' until you are fully recovered from this ill turn. Are you able to walk, with my support? It is only a few steps, you know."

"I will try," she briefly replied.

CHAPTER XV.

MISS LAMPSON AMAZED.

He gently but firmly lifted her from her chair anxious to get her away from the curious eyes of the crowd that was beginning to gather about them, and, drawing her hand through his arm, conducted her from the place, and down toward "The Antlers."

She appeared outwardly composed to the casual observer; but her face was like alabaster, and she was trembling in every limb.

Mr. Lancaster himself was scarcely less unnerved than she, for he knew that there were problems staring him in the face—problems that would not be easy to solve—and a sense of guilt and humiliation almost overpowered him.

For one thing, and standing out more clearly than all others, was the fact that he had repudiated and scorned the child of the woman whom he had loved all his life. He had regarded her as of too common clay to mate with his nephew. Too common! Ah, Heaven! What would she think of him, if she should ever learn how he had plotted and schemed to ruin her happiness?

What would Bob think and say, if he should ever discover how he had bribed Hubert Alton to marry the girl he loved, for the sake of getting her out of his reach? While, of course, he had no means of knowing what schemes he might have resorted to to achieve his purpose. He had often felt heart-sick, in view of these thoughts. At all events, it was evident that those schemes had been thwarted, and the girl had probably been saved from a lifetime of misery; and now, in view of the appalling discovery which he had made to-day, he was so supremely grateful, he felt that he could almost have fallen upon his knees, and kissed the feet of whoever had interposed to rescue her.

If the explanations, which he had determined should follow this meeting with Margaret, should bring to light all that he now so much regretted, would the lovely girl turn from him with loathing? Would Bob hate him forever afterward? These were not pleasant possibilities to contemplate.

He spoke to his companion only once on their way to the hotel, and that was just as they were about to enter the house.

"Margaret," he said humbly, "I can see that my presence is exceedingly repugnant to you; but promise that you will listen patiently to me for a few moments; I beg, I entreat!" he concluded with despairing earnestness.

She turned, and lifted her eyes to his face.

Its pallor, its tenderness, its humility and despair appealed to her with such force that tears gathered in them, and her voice was very sweet and gentle, as she replied:

"Yes; I will listen to what you have to say, for—I am afraid that I have not been quite just to you."

Ah, the magic of those last words!

They made a new man of Halburton Lancaster!

He straightened himself, threw back his stalwart shoulders, drawing in a deep breath, and a look of triumph swept into his eyes, and glorified his whole face.

He felt, after that confession, that she would, at least, forgive him the wrongs of the past.

He involuntarily drew the hand that rested upon his arm close to his side, then led her within the hotel, and to a small reception-room, which he hoped to find empty.

But he was doomed to disappointment, for the first person he saw there was the voluble Miss Lampson, who, with some of the other boarders from Crescent Villa, had gathered there to discuss the events of the day with some of the guests of "The Antlers."

Most of them were people whom Mrs. Seymour knew, and they all stared with astonishment as she entered the room with her distinguished-looking companion.

"This will never do," said Mr. Lancaster, as he led her to a corner, and found her a chair; "we cannot talk here. I will go to the office, to see if I can obtain a private parlor."

He bowed courteously to her as he turned and left her, and presently Miss Lampson, whose curiosity could no longer be controlled, and which was only equaled by her audacity, left her companions, made her way to her side, and observed, in an insinuating tone, while she searched her still pale face with her keen eyes:

"Were you in the accident, Mrs. Seymour? Were you injured?"

"No—oh, no; I was simply frightened, and somewhat overcome by—the excitement," Mrs. Seymour quietly replied, but with an air which plainly indicated that she did not care to pursue the conversation further.

The spinster was piqued by her manner, but she had no idea of being driven from the field without making a strenuous effort to ascertain what she wanted to know.

She had always been jealous of the woman's beauty, as well as of her costumes, which, although they did not exceed her own in richness of materials, nevertheless had a certain style and grace which she could never, with her figure, hope to copy. More than this, she was conscious of, and hated her for, her intellectual and moral superiority.

"It was a fine show, wasn't it?" she went on airily, and regardless, apparently, of her coldness; "the finest we've ever had yet, and I've seen every one since they were first started."

"Ah!" absently observed her listener.

"Yes; there were more truly artistic designs than ever before. The Wallace trap, for instance, was lovely, and I was told that you had a hand in that; and it really was like your dainty taste."

The lie was uttered glibly enough, for she had been told nothing of the kind; she had simply assumed it, for the sake of learning the truth.

"Yes?" was the non-committal response that made the spinster's eyes flash angrily, and she immediately bridled to shoot an arrow that should tell.

"The girls looked lovely," she began, with a sweetly patronizing air; "their beautiful white costumes and dead-black hats, against the background of green, were exceedingly effective. But, really, Mrs. Seymour"—in a tone of grave surprise—"I wonder that you could have allowed Helen to appear so conspicuously in the parade, after——"

"After what, Miss Lampson?" demanded Mrs. Seymour, with an air and in a tone that made the malicious woman wince, in spite of her effrontery, while she arose and stood tall, and straight, and imposing, before her.

And, just at that moment, she espied Mr. Lancaster, standing in the doorway, and wondered what could have caused the stern compression of his lips and the flash of fire in his eyes.

He had been obliged to pause for a moment there, for a knot of ladies barred his way, and were so absorbed in what they were saying they did not observe that he was there, overhearing that which made his blood boil and tingle with indignation to his very finger-tips.

"Yes," said the spokesman of the group. "Miss Lampson says that Mrs. Ellsworth has known her ever since she was a girl, and that she isn't what she pretends at all—that she really is a disreputable character——"

"Ah! I heard something about that myself," interposed a little woman in an eager tone, "but she is such a beautiful-looking woman, and seems so refined, I could hardly credit it."

"Well, but it's true all the same," was the response, "for Mrs. Ellsworth says her name isn't Seymour at all, and that the girl never had a father. Just think of it! And she riding in the procession to-day in such a brazen way!"

Mr. Lancaster waited to hear no more, but, with blazing eyes and a face almost as white as his hair, pushed his way through the group toward Mrs. Seymour, who, with a red spot on either cheek, was waiting Miss Lampson's reply to her question.

"Why—I shouldn't think you'd need to ask—after all that has been said about you and her," was the sharp and insulting retort, which also fell upon Mr. Lancaster's ears as he drew near. Miss Lampson saw him at that instant, and something in his face made her quake inwardly.

"Why!" she exclaimed, hardly conscious of what she was saying; "are you acquainted with Mrs. Seymour, Mr. Lancaster?" I—I saw you helping her out of the crowd, but I didn't suppose you knew each other."

The gentleman had removed his hat upon entering the room, and now stood towering aloft beside the woman he adored, his splendid figure, his fine head crowned with its abundant snow-white hair, making him one to be singled out among a thousand.

"Yes," he replied to the disconcerted woman before him, his tones clear and incisive, his words crisp and curt, and heard by every one in the room, upon which a sudden hush had fallen. "I have known this lady for more than twenty years; she is—my wife, madam!"

Had a thunderbolt fallen in their midst, the result could not have been more paralyzing.

A hush like that of death settled over the group of gossips, every one of whom had learned something of the wealthy and distinguished Mr. Lancaster, and his enviable position in the world; and every face had grown blank and gray from mingled astonishment and consternation when that astounding and triumphant declaration had fallen upon their ears.

As for Miss Lampson, the wind had been so completely taken out of her sails, she collapsed utterly, and sank weakly upon the nearest chair, her head spinning like a top.

One by one, her companions stole silently away, until she was left alone with the woman whom she had so cruelly traduced and the man who had so nobly—though daringly—defended her.

"Yes," continued Mr. Lancaster, sternly, when he saw they were alone, "this dear woman, whom you have known as Mrs. Seymour, has been my wife more than a score of years, Miss Lampson!" with scathing and significant emphasis; "you have sneeringly and maliciously proclaimed that she had no right to the name by which she has chosen to call herself; you have dared to assert even worse things of her and her beautiful daughter; but—how is it about the one you are yourself bearing? Perhaps it will be as well for your own reputation if you refrain hereafter from rehearsing this foul scandal, which you have learned from unreliable sources. Come, Margaret," he con-

cluded in a tone of infinite tenderness, as he gently
took one of her hands and drew it within his arm,
then led her from the room, leaving the other woman
sitting limp and white, and looking as if her doom
had been pronounced upon her.

Mr. Lancaster conducted his companion along a
wide hall, until he came to an open door on the right.

"In here," he briefly said, and ushered her into a
pretty apartment that looked out upon the spacious
grounds behind the hotel, and also off upon the grand
peaks beyond.

He closed and locked the door, then turned, and
opened his arms to the trembling woman beside him.

"I have dared to claim you, my darling, in the face
of all the world!" he said in husky tones; "have I been
too bold and presumptuous? Will you come?"

He was frightfully pale, and trembled like a reed.

Margaret Seymour put out her shaking hands to
him.

"Hal!" she sobbed. "Oh, Hal!" You do believe in
me, after all?"

"Believe in you, my own!" he cried, as he drew her
to his breast, and held her close. "I know—I always
knew—that you were the purest woman on God's
earth! Oh, forgive me, that I ever seemed to doubt
you, even for a moment! See, dear"—and he lifted
one of her hands to his own white head—"this was
blanched in less than a month from grief and remorse
for having so wronged you."

Then the strong man broke down utterly, and
sobbed like a child, for the pent-up loneliness, the
wretchedness and yearning of more than twenty years
were unlocked in that moment of blessed reunion,
and the reaction was more than he could meet with
calmness.

And Margaret lay upon his breast, restful and content, like a tired, wandering child that at last has

found its home; and, although tears were raining over her own cheeks, there were tremulous smiles on her lips, and a light in her eyes that had not gleamed there for many years.

At last, she lifted her hand, and, with her own handkerchief, softly wiped the great drops from his face.

The tender act touched him more than anything else could have done, comforting him beyond measure, and assured him that he was forgiven—that all the bitterness of the past was forever blotted out from her book of remembrance.

He lifted her face, and showered passionate kisses upon her brow, cheeks, and lips, calling her by the old-time sweet, tender names that he had been wont to use in the days of their early married life.

At length, he led her to a divan, and drew her down beside him, but still keeping his arms about her.

"I have sought you everywhere, my darling, and yet I hardly dared to hope that you would forgive me, even if I succeeded in finding you," he murmured, while his hungry eyes feasted themselves upon the beautiful face that was resting upon his shoulder.

"And I believed that I never could forgive you, Hal, until after a fearful illness brought me very near death's door, a year ago last winter," she gravely returned. "It was a long, long sickness, and I had time to think, and, in my weakness, the desolateness and loneliness of the past seemed intensified a hundredfold, and I began to realize that I had never ceased to yearn for you, in spite of the fact that I had continually nursed my bitterness against you. I realized, also, that I myself needed to be forgiven for having left you in the way I did—without one word of warning regarding my intention."

"Ah, sweetheart, the suspense—the uncertainty

have been something terrible!" said her husband, with a shiver at the recollection of what he had suffered.

"I know," she returned regretfully; "but, then, in my pain and resentment after that dreadful day, I did not stop to consider that you, also, would suffer, when you came to yourself, and knew that I had never been untrue, or that you would be anxious regarding my future. And afterward, when I learned the fact myself, as I soon did, I was still too proud and obstinate to do what conscience told me was my duty, and inform you that a little one would some day come to me."

"Ah! You refer to Helen—your daughter and mine!" he said, as she paused and lifted a repentant look to him.

"Yes; but how did you know that?" she questioned in surprise.

"I never knew it until this day—almost this hour—that she was your child—our child," he replied, barely repressing a groan as he thought of his sin against the fair girl.

"But how did you learn the fact to-day? Who told you, Hal? How did you know I was in the stand? How happen to come to me as you did? It all seems very strange and mysterious to me," said Margaret, looking perplexed.

"Well, it all came about through that Lampson woman, and, though I think she is despicable, perhaps I ought to feel grateful to her, for I might not have seen you if she had not pointed you out to me. She sat in the box next to the one I occupied during the parade—I knew her years ago, during my youth—we recognized each other, and then she told me something about the people in the various traps. When the Wallace equipage passed, I recognized Helen instantly——"

"Why! How could that be possible?" queried Mrs.

Lancaster—as we shall hereafter call her—more astonished than ever. "You could never have met her before!"

"Yes; I saw her at a school reception, after Rob's graduation; then again, four years later, in Central Park."

"In Central Park?"

"Yes; she had a fall from her horse there, and I assisted her to remount. Did she never tell you?"

"No," said Mrs. Lancaster, paling slightly in view of the accident.

"I suppose she did not like to speak of it, and, she was not hurt at all, it did not matter; but, of course, when I saw her to-day, I knew her instantly as Miss Helen Seymour, although I did not know then who she really was," Mr. Lancaster explained.

"And Miss Lampson pointed me out to you! Did she also regale you——"

"Yes; she had plenty of boarding-house gossip at her tongue's end when Helen came riding by, and then said she would show me her mother," Mr. Lancaster went on. "When I got a glimpse of you, between the teams, the truth burst upon me with stunning force. I knew you at once—you have not changed much, dear, except to grow a hundredfold more lovely—and, then I also knew who Helen was—what she was to me—and, oh, I cannot begin to comprehend, even yet, all that the fact involves!" concluded the man, with quivering lips and in a heart-broken tone.

"But you have long known that Rob wanted to marry Helen Seymour?" said Margaret, lifting her head from his breast, to search his face; "and you did not want him to marry her!"

"That is true, I am forced to admit; but, of course, I never dreamed that it was my own daughter whom he wished to marry!" he groaned, as he recalled that interview with Rob, more than two years previous, during which he had said such slighting things about the "fashionable dressmaker" and her daughter, and about his marrying beneath his own position in life, as he remembered again the bribe he had offered Hubert Alton to win the girl from her lover.

He felt crushed to the earth, in view of the humiliating situation in which he found himself. Surely, his sin had found him out, and his punishment seemed greater than he could bear.

He had yielded to an unworthy temptation to save Rob from what he had supposed would be a great mésalliance; he had tempted another to sin—perhaps even to the verge of crime, and thus he had unwittingly wronged those nearest and dearest to himself.

How could he ever face his lovely daughter, he wondered. How much did she and her mother know regarding his agency in the separation of herself and Rob? And, if they knew the whole story, how could he ever set himself right with them? It seemed to him that he had sinned beyond the power of reparation.

But he did not mean to commit himself more than was necessary until he found that confession was inevitable, and so he asked, with fear and trembling:

"And you, sweetheart, did you know that it was my boy whom Helen loved?"

"No; not until you had been abroad for more than a year," his wife returned. "Of course, Rob came often to the house, for a long time before he went away, and he used to speak of you always as 'my uncle.' I, with my many cares, never thought to inquire particularly about you. I took it for granted that your name was the same as his, and supposed that you were the noted Dr. Eggleston. I was very remiss, I admit, but Rob and Helen were young, and I did not dream that matters had gone as far as they had, until just before Rob sailed, when he asked me to sanction his love for Helen."

"Ah!" Did he go as far as that?" queried Mr. Lancaster, with an inward start.

"Yes; and I then asked him how his uncle regarded the situation. He said that he had spoken with you, and you had said, if they were both of the same mind on his return, you would consent to the union. I was, somehow, impressed, even then, that there was something back of that condition—that you were opposed to the alliance, and I immediately adopted the same attitude. I would consent to no engagement until his return, although I liked the young man right well. It was only after the Ellsworths joined the party, and Marjorie—who corresponded regularly with Helen—wrote of you as Mr. Lancaster—Halburton Lancaster—and Rob's uncle, that I learned the truth, and recognized the wisdom of my decision, although I knew that you could have no suspicion that Helen Seymour's mother was your wife of twenty-one years previous.

"I was appalled by the fact that we two had been living in the same city for so long! How strange that we never chanced to meet!" she concluded musingly.

CHAPTER XVI.

HUSBAND AND WIFE.

"It is, indeed! And—I suppose, when you learned the truth, you had to tell Helen?" began Mr. Lancaster, a gleam of pain in his eyes.

"No; I did not."

"Love! You have never told her? She does not know that I am her father?"

"No; I could not tell her," said the fair woman, with a sigh. "I had always allowed her to believe that her father had died before she was born, and that her name was Seymour. When she questioned me, I always said that I lost him several months previous to that event; and, to me, you were the same as dead, for I never supposed that we would be reunited. I felt confident that, if she should learn her real name, and that you were still living, she would know no rest until she had searched you out, for she has always grieved because she has had no father like other girls. After that letter from Marjorie came, and I learned who Rob's uncle was, the knowledge was too much for me—it was like an unexpected blow from a hammer, and I fainted. When I recovered, Helen demanded an explanation, but I simply told her that I had suffered wrong through you in my youth—in fact," Mrs. Lancaster interposed, flushing; "I told her something of my story, but in a way to make it appear that you were the one who had made trouble between me and my husband. I could not tell her, Hal, that you were her father, and had believed that her mother had been false to you," she faltered.

"Hush, dearest! I knew in my heart, even in that supreme moment, that you were true," said Mr. Lancaster, as he checked her with a reverent kiss; "but, in my madness, in my insane jealousy over what I had heard from time to time, and upon finding my worst fears confirmed by the presence of John Wilton in your private parlor, I lost my head, and said things that I bitterly regretted—yea, cursed myself for—not twenty-four hours afterward. But it was too late then to redeem myself, for you were gone. By the way, where is your cousin, Margaret? Have you even seen him? Do you know anything of his career?"

"Yes; I met John very unexpectedly two years ago—the only time I have seen him during all these years," his wife returned. "We were spending a few weeks in the Adirondacks. I started out one morning for a tramp in the woods, when he came upon me suddenly. We were both upset, for, of course, it brought everything freshly to our minds. He seemed very humble and repentant because of his share in my trouble; and, when he learned how I had lived since leaving my home, he wanted to share his wealth with me. He said he had plenty of money, and no one upon whom to spend it, and that I had a right to it. I suppose, being his nearest of kin, that was true; besides, you know, his father was my father's brother, and he always had a home with us after he was left an orphan, until he went out into the world for himself."

"And you would not allow him to provide for you, Margaret?" questioned her husband.

"No; I needed no help at that time, for I had been doing a prosperous business for years; but, even if I had been in bitter need, I could never have taken his money, for it was through him, and his mad folly, that I lost all that I prised most in my life."

"Ah, dearest, you have had a sad experience!" said Mr. Lancaster, as he drew her closer within his protecting arms. "My love! my love! It pierces me to my soul to know that you have suffered poverty and hardship when I have had riches to spare. Margaret, it was wrong, cruel, to deprive yourself and our child of your rightful heritage."

"Yes; I have come to see many things differently since I have been ill," said the fair woman, with a regretful sigh, "but what has troubled me most, is the fact that I have kept you in ignorance of Helen's existence during all these years."

"Oh! If I had only known the truth!" groaned the man, with a sudden rush of despair, as he thought of the evil that he had perpetrated against his own daughter.

"Forgive me, Hal!" pleaded Margaret humbly, as he lifted her tear-wet face to him, and laid her lips against his. "I wish now—oh, how I wish!—that I had not been so rash in the long ago. How keenly one realizes and regrets one's mistakes as one grows older, and looks back upon them from a different point of view."

"You shall not blame yourself, my darling!" cried her husband passionately. "I am the one who should reproach myself. If I had only been calm—if I had not allowed my anger and jealousy to get the better of me, but had investigated matters in a reasonable and dispassionate way, all our sorrows and long separation might have been avoided."

"And yet, Hal, you must go back of even that for the cause of it all," said his companion gravely, "for we were both the victims of that treacherous girl whom we befriended."

"I do not quite understand you, dear," said Mr. Lancaster, with a look of perplexity.

"Do you not know—have you never suspected—that

Marien Waldbridge—now—Marien Ellsworth—deliberately planned to ruin me?"

"No!"

"It is true," pursued his wife. "From the day when she first met my cousin, John Wilton, who used to come to see me occasionally at school, she loved him, and used all her arts to win him. But, you know, he had been fond of me for years, and, as long as I was single, he would not give up the hope of winning me. Even after we were married, he so enraged Marien by persisting in showing me devoted attention that she grew to hate me with all her heart. Her aim evidently was to create a scandal that would ruin my reputation with the world, and make such a breach between us and John Wilton that he would turn to her for comfort, and thus she would eventually win him. I know how artfully she insinuated, in that innocent way of hers, that I was not quite open in all my doings —how she attracted your attention to little things that were nothing in themselves, to arouse your suspicion that I favored John more than I ought. I know she made him believe that I was not happy with you, and regretted that I had not chosen differently, and that was why he persisted in seeking me as he did. She sent him a message that day, telling him that I wanted to see him—watched for his coming, then, instead of having me go down to receive him in the drawing-room, conducted him, as if by appointment, up to my private parlor, and I knew absolutely nothing of the matter until he stood in my presence. Immediately afterward, she sent you a cunning message, which excited your suspicions that something was very wrong."

"Margaret! I can scarcely credit my ears! How did you learn all this?" exclaimed Mr. Lancaster in astonishment. "Why, I supposed—until recently—that Marien Waldbridge loved you as a sister? She certainly manifested almost uncontrollable grief upon learning of your disappearance."

"Yes, I know; she acted her part to perfection; she even deceived me, up to almost the last moment," returned Margaret, with a weary sigh; "but John's suspicions were aroused as soon as you appeared upon the scene. He had long known that Marien loved him, and was jealous of me, and, after that dreadful scene, after you and I had both left the room, she went to him, as a pretended comforter. Then he turned upon her, and charged her with the whole scheme. They were both so angry that I could easily hear all that was said from my chamber. At first, she tried to deny everything, but he dissected the plot, point by point, making her contradict herself time and again, and finally cornered her so cleverly that she broke down entirely, and owned up everything, but pleaded her love for him as her excuse. His denunciation of her was something terrible. He told her, among other things, that, through her meanness and treachery, she had caused him to irreparably wrong the only woman whose esteem and respect, above all others, he cared to preserve, vowed that he would never recognize her again as long as he lived, and turned and left her."

"Oh, my darling, when you learned that all that terrible misunderstanding had been brought about by her treachery, why could you not have come to me, and revealed the fact?" groaned the remorseful man.

"Because I was beside myself. I was, for the time being, driven almost insane by your distrust of me!" Margaret sobbed. "I told myself you had no right to believe that your wife, who loved you as I loved, who had chosen you from all the world, could be unfaithful to you. I said that you knew I lived but for you, and that our home was my sanctuary, my holy of holies; that you should have known that it was as impossible for me to wrong you so as for the sun to be put out, and I vowed that I would never forgive you. John, also, I swore never to pardon, for he should have known better than to have supposed, for one moment, that, even if I had not been happy with you, I could so dishonor myself as to listen to professions of love from another man, and prove false to my vows to my husband. I felt that he had offered me an irreparable insult, for I had never given him the slightest encouragement to believe that I entertained any but a cousinly regard for him after I became engaged to you. And so, in my folly and madness, thinking only of myself, my individual sufferings and wrongs, I packed a few necessary articles of clothing, and stole away as soon as night came on."

"Oh, Margaret! Margaret! Think of all those lost years!"

"I know; I can see now that I was selfish and inconsiderate, and I was soon to reap the punishment for my wickedness, for"—hiding her face again upon his breast— "when it dawned upon me that I was to become a mother, I knew that I had done you and our little one the greatest possible wrong, and, realizing the poverty, desolation, and helplessness that were before me, I was, for a time, in the depths of despair. But, even then, I was so proud and obstinate that I could not bring myself to send for you—to confess my wrong, and sue for your love, pardon, and protection, for a spirit of evil whispered to me that you might not receive me, and my proud spirit would never brook repudiation; besides, I was three thousand miles from you, as I supposed, having come straight on to New York from California, and I had no means of knowing that you had not already taken steps to free yourself from the tie that bound us."

"Never, sweetheart! Such a thought never tempted me for a moment," earnestly returned her husband.

"My only hope was to find you, and plead for pardon for my momentary distrust of you. I first sought you in the west—advertised in all the papers, traveled hundreds of miles, going to every place where we had ever been. Then, after a year of this hopeless search, I closed up my business, and came East. Then I was called South, to my step-sister, who was slowly dying, and who committed her child to me to rear and educate. I was too heart-sick to go back to our old home, for I knew it would be desolate without you, so I started business in New York, hoping that the hurry and bustle of the great city would help to drown my sorrow."

"And you have lived there ever since?" questioned the wife, with a heart-broken sob.

"Yes, with the exception of a portion of every year, which I spent at the old homestead, in Virginia, which I inherited from my father, and which demanded my personal attention."

"And I was there, too, struggling for my daily bread! And we never met! How cruel fate has been! How I have been punished for my folly!" and the long-tried woman broke down again, overcome by the sad memories and regrets that thronged upon her.

Mr. Lancaster folded her closer to him, while he tenderly wiped the tears that rained over her cheeks.

"My poor darling, I cannot be reconciled to it!" he said, with deep emotion. "Surely, that woman will have much to answer for," he continued, as his thoughts turned to Marien Ellsworth. "We three— you, John, and I—were indeed poor, deluded mortals —victims of a moral leper.

"Heavens!" he added, mentally, and with a sense of loathing; "and to think that she has been plotting to entangle me again in her toils within the last year! She, too, supposed I had been divorced, and hoped to marry me, and so retrieve her fallen fortunes. How quickly she showed out her spite, that night in Calcutta, when I whispered to her that I was still bound to Margaret, living or dead."

"Of what are you thinking, Hal?" questioned his wife, wondering at his silence, and the peculiar expression on his face.

Mr. Lancaster started slightly. Bad as he now knew Marien Ellsworth to have been he felt that he owed her much, because of her care of Rob during that terrible illness, and he shrank from betraying, even to his wife, how lost she had been to all womanly delicacy in asking him to marry her.

"Well," he replied, with a smile, "a thousand thoughts are teeming in my brain, and among them the feeling that I have, perhaps, been rather hard upon John, for, although he had no right to make love to you while you were my wife, I can now see that he was really more sinned against than sinning."

"Yes, during the last year, I, too, have felt more lenient toward him," Margaret responded.

And so they talked on for more than an hour, and, even then, there was much that still remained to be explained.

But, all at once, Mrs. Lancaster remembered that her friends, the Wallaces, did not know where she was, and would be anxious about her.

"I really must not remain here any longer, Hal," she said, sitting up, and glancing at her watch. "It is after five o'clock, and Helen and my friends will wonder what has become of me."

"But, dearest, you are mine once more; we will never be separated again!" said Mr. Lancaster, gently detaining her within his encircling arms, and searching her face with inquiring eyes.

"No, Hal; and"—nestling closer to him—"I am so thankful that we are reunited at last. I have been unutterably desolate all these years without you."

"Desolate! Love, the word will not begin to express what I have suffered!" said the man, with trembling lips. "Had it not been for Rob, I should have had absolutely no object in life, save that of making money. And Helen," he added, "do you suppose she will accept and love me as her father? Will she forgive me, I wonder, for carrying off her lover? For with shame, I confess it, Margaret, I—I wasn't quite willing that my dear boy should marry a dressmaker's daughter."

He tried to smile, and speak lightly, as he said it; but he was groaning in spirit with anguish, in view of what else he had done.

"But you had told Rob you would not object to his choice, if they were both of the same mind on his return, you know," said his wife, eager to accord him all due charity.

Mr. Lancaster flushed. He knew he had not committed himself to that extent; he had told him that, if he was of the same mind on his return, there would be ample time then to settle the question of his marriage.

"Well, I am sure Rob gave up all hope of winning her long ago," he said evasively, "for we heard, last summer, through letters from our firm, that she was going to marry one of my clerks—Hubert Alton."

"Yes, that was true," Mrs. Lancaster gravely returned, "but Helen had first been led to believe that Rob had changed his mind, and was going to marry Marjorie Ellsworth."

"What on earth gave her such an impression?" exclaimed the gentleman in astonismhent.

"She was led to infer as much from Marjorie's letters."

"Ah! So the girl has some of her mother's craftiness in her composition—she is not quite as artless as she seems!" said Mr. Lancaster, his face darkening, for he had really been very fond of Marjorie, and it pained him to learn that she had been so deceptive, for he well knew that she had had no authority to represent that Rob had any matrimonial intentions regarding herself.

"I have had my own suspicions to that effect," said Mrs. Lancaster, "but Helen still believes in her. Regarding Helen's contemplated marriage with Hubert Alton, she was literally driven to it to save my life, for we had lost almost all I had accumulated, and the doctor said I would surely die if I remained in the hot city during the summer. Hubert had long been fond of Helen, and wanted to marry her, but she would not listen to him, until, in our extremity, he offered to provide a home for us in the country. There seemed to be no other resort, and she yielded. Then, oh, we had a perfectly dreadful time!"

"Again?" groaned her husband.

"Yes; it all came out right, though. But—really Hal, I must go now; cannot you come with me, and I will tell you about it on our way to Mr. Wallace's, where we are expected to dine."

The man was very pale; he was wondering what more of evil he was about to learn to add to his punishment, which already seemed heavier than he could bear, in spite of the great happiness that had come to him that day.

But he arose, at his wife's suggestion, and touched an electric button.

"Yes, dear," he said. "I will order a carriage, and drive you myself. I cannot let you out of my sight until I am absolutely obliged to do so."

"I might send to ask Mrs. Wallace to excuse me, and for Helen to come to us, if you think best," said Margaret musingly, "but it would break up their dinner party, and I would like to see Helen alone, and tell her something more of my past before she meets you; it would be quite a shock, I think, to tell her suddenly."

"I think it would be hardly fair to disappoint the Wallaces, much as I dislike to give you up, even for an hour," said her husband. "So I will take you to them, and we will arrange on our way for a later meeting."

In less than ten minutes, the carriage was at the door, and the reunited husband and wife rode away, with a light on their faces that had not rested there for many years.

During their drive, which covered nearly two miles, the home of the Wallaces being pretty well out on Cascade Avenue, Mrs. Lancaster related in detail the incidents that had led up to Helen's proposed marriage with Hubert Alton, together with the startling dénouement which had so changed everything, and released the devoted girl from a fate which, she had since confessed, would have been a wretched, and almost insupportable, bondage to her.

"Well, I am amazed!" exclaimed Mr. Lancaster, as she concluded. "It seems like a wonderful interposition of Providence, that that girl should have appeared upon the scene, with her baby, just at that time! And—and—what became of the young man afterward?"

"I do not know; we have never seen or heard anything of him since. We hear from Mary occasionally, and she is still living in our little suite, keeping house for Mr. Smith and his protégé. She writes that he is more than kind to her, and she cannot say enough in his praise. I think he must be a fine man—he is certainly honorable, for we still receive our check in advance as regularly as the first day of the month comes around."

"God bless Mr. Smith, and that other man, who purchased your cottage so opportunely!" said Mr. Lancaster heartily, and little thinking upon whom he was invoking a benediction. "But," he added, with a frown, as his mind reverted to Hubert Alton, and the girl whom he had wronged, "we shall have to look into that matter, and see if we cannot set Mary Wadleigh and her child right."

"Ah, that would be such a blessing to the poor girl," sighed Mrs. Lancaster; then added, as she indicated a residence on the right that they were approaching: "This is the house, dear," and Mr. Lancaster immediately drew up before it.

CHAPTER XVII.

ENIGMAS.

Mrs. Wallace, with her two younger daughters, was sitting upon the veranda, and they all arose and went down the steps to greet Mrs. Lancaster, as she alighted from the carriage.

"Oh, Mrs. Seymour!" exclaimed her hostess in a tone of intense relief. "I am more thankful than I can express to have you safely here once more! We were very anxious about you. Mr. Wallace went to the grand stand to look for you after we were safely out, but failed to find you. Then he thought best to bring us home, as we were all pretty well used up from the fright we had received. He returned immediately, however, to seek for you. Have you seen nothing of him, or the girls?"

"No; and I am very sorry that you were so disturbed," Mrs. Lancaster replied. "I have been well cared for," she added, with a smile, "for my—an old friend came to my assistance, and took me to 'The Antlers' to rest, after which he kindly brought me home."

She here introduced Mr. Lancaster, but did not betray their relationship, as they had agreed, before alighting, that Helen should be taken into the secret first, the situation thoroughly understood and discussed before allowing anything in their history to be known to the world.

Mrs. Lancaster said she would like to give Mrs. Wallace a hint as to how matters stood before she left that evening, for she had been so very kind to her during her recent trying experience in Colorado Springs.

She knew that she could say nothing to Helen until they could be alone together; accordingly, she planned to return to her boarding-place as soon after dinner with her friends as courtesy would allow, and break the news to her.

Mr. Lancaster, meantime, was to have an interview with Rob, explain everything to him, and bring him around to Mrs. Forsyth's between eight and nine.

Mrs. Wallace hospitably invited Mr. Lancaster to come in and join the family at dinner, but he excused himself, saying that he had an important commission to execute, and then, after chatting a few moments in a general way, he bade the ladies "Good evening," and drove away.

He had ridden only a block or two down the avenue, when he met Miss Wallace and Helen, on their way home, their bright faces plainly indicating that they were in their happiest frame of mind.

He lifted his hat, in courteous recognition, and smiled congratulations at the white satin banner waving above them, although his glance lingered yearningly upon Helen's lovely face.

The girl knew him instantly, and what color she had regained while riding about with her friend faded at once from her cheeks; but she did not acknowledge his greeting, although Hetty smiled, and bowed graciously, for a feeling of fierce resentment arose in her heart against him as she thought of a certain letter and telegram that were, at that moment, lying at the bottom of her writing-desk at Mrs. Forsyth's.

Mr. Lancaster's heart sank at the cut he had received, and which was all the more noticeable because of Miss Wallace's graciousness.

"She, as well as her mother, feels that I took Rob

away with a purpose," he muttered in a despondent tone.

But he did not dream how much more she knew.

He was satisfied that his wife had no knowledge whatever regarding his negotiations with Hubert Alton, for he reasoned that, if one had learned the truth, the other must have also become cognizant of it, and he devoutly hoped that it would forever remain a secret between himself and the young man.

Helen was still very pale when she alighted from the trap before the Wallaces' door, and mounted the steps with her friend to join the party on the veranda.

But, in spite of the tumult within her own heart, she was instantly attracted by her mother's bright face and shining eyes, and, when she laughed out heartily at a droll incident that Hetty was relating, she detected a peculiar ring of joyousness in the tones, and marveled, for she did not remember ever having heard her laugh so merrily before.

"Well, young ladies, I am glad you have enjoyed yourselves so thoroughly, and you have certainly been greatly honored," she smilingly observed, as she nodded at them, and glanced approvingly at the banner. Then, observing Helen's pallor, she inquired anxiously: "What is it, dear? Have you been getting too tired?"

"I'm afraid Helen isn't quite well," Hetty observed, before the girl could reply. "She had a fainting turn just as we were leaving the grand stand, and she has not seemed like herself since, in spite of the fact that we have been driving about for more than an hour, waving our banner, and glorying in our triumph," she concluded, with dancing eyes and a grandiloquent air.

"Oh, it was nothing," Helen hastened to say reassuringly, and smiling into her mother's questioning eyes; "just a momentary feeling of dizziness. But wasn't it a lovely sight, mamma?" she went on, to distract attention from herself. "It went far beyond my wildest expectations—it was like a gorgeous fairytale; and to think that we won this lovely trophy!" waving the banner gaily aloft. "Isn't Hetty a lucky girl?"

"I really think we ought to have had two,". Miss Hetty observed, and assuming a grieved look that evoked shouts of derisive laughter from her companions, "for then we could each have one, and I feel awfully mean to keep this all to myself, especially"—with a deprecatory glance at Mrs. Lancaster—"when the credit of that beautiful, fairy-like vehicle out there does not belong to me."

Mrs. Lancaster arose, and, going to the girl's side, passed one arm around her waist.

"My dear," she said tremulously, "all credit belongs to you and your dear, good mother. Do you suppose I do not know and appreciate why you have all been so more than kind to us during the last two or three weeks?"

Hetty flushed to her temples at this unexpected tribute, and glanced helplessly at her mother, who also changed color slightly.

"My dear friend," said Mrs. Wallace, coming to her daughter's rescue, "pray do not attribute more to us than we deserve, for, I assure you, we have cultivated your friendship and Helen's because of your own intrinsic worth and our enjoyment of your society. Of course, I understand to what you refer—our loyalty to you in a time of trial—and, if we have taken especial pains to show it before others, I hope you will feel that it was only because we appreciate you both for what you are."

"All the same, we are none the less greateful for the moral courage you have manifested, and the delicate way in which you have made it apparent to others," said Mrs. Lancaster, with evident emotion.

"I am satisfied with the result," returned Mrs. Wallace, smiling fondly into Helen's grave eyes, "and I am sure there were some mischief-makers there to-day who will wish they hadn't been quite such busy-bodies in other people's affairs. Ah, here comes Mr. Wallace!" she added, as the gentleman wheeled into the driveway; "and I know, by his face, that he is greatly relieved to find his whole party here safe and sound."

The gentleman waved a smiling greeting to the group on the veranda, then drove on to the stable, just as a groom came to take the span of blacks and the trap to the same place.

Miss Hetty watched the turnout with regretful eyes.

"It is too pretty to be dismantled," she said with a sigh; "but I know it will all be withered and faded by to-morrow."

"The memory of it—of this beautiful day, and all that it has meant to me, will never fade from my heart, Hetty, dear," said Helen, as she lifted her eyes, that were full of tears, to her friend.

Mrs. Wallace now arose from her chair.

"Come," she said to Mrs. Lancaster, "let us go in, and remove our hats, for dinner will be served immediately, now that Mr. Wallace has come. Hetty, of course, you will take care of Helen."

She led the way to her own room, and, while they were there, Mrs. Lancaster took the opportunity to tell her briefly something of what had occurred that afternoon, and that, after many long years of separation, she had, at last been reunited to her husband—the gentleman who had escorted her hither half-an-hour previous.

Mrs. Wallace, although greatly astonished, was truly glad for her.

"How rejoiced I am!" she exclaimed; "and I have been sure that, if there was a mystery connected with your life, as has been said, it could be nothing detrimental to you, all vulgar gossip to the contrary notwithstanding. How I wish I had known, and could have kept Mr. Lancaster to dinner," she concluded, with hospitable regret.

"But Helen does not know yet," returned her guest; "and we both felt that this was no time for general explanations. I am going to ask you to excuse us very soon after dinner, for you can understand that there is yet much to be told, and my husband is eager to have us with him."

"Indeed, I can understand, and I also feel that you are very self-sacrificing to remain with us to dinner, rather than disarrange and deplete our party," said Mrs. Wallace, appreciatively. "Ah!" she continued, smiling; "I do not wonder that you are looking almost like a young girl, with this lovely color in your cheeks, and that new light of hope and joy shining in your eyes; and you must tell me all the romance of your life later on."

"Indeed, I will, gladly; I owe you a great deal, dear Mrs. Wallace, for your brave championship in the face of adverse public opinion," was the grateful reply.

"Don't mention it! I simply detest vulgar gossip, and I have always set my face steadfastly against it; but I have seldom come out so triumphantly as I seem likely to in this case of 'championship,' as you are pleased to term it," said the lady, with a little exultant laugh, as she thought of what a reaction there would be when Mrs. Lancaster's story became known.

The dinner passed off delightfully, for every one, unless we except Helen, was in high spirits, Mr. Wallace being especially hilarious, in view of his daughter's signal triumph that afternoon.

"It really was the prettiest thing on wheels to-day," he said in a gratified tone, "and I flatter myself that the horses were, at least, a match for any span in the parade, while Mehetable, my child, you did yourself proud with the ribbons."

"Thank you, papa," said Hetty, flushing, and laughing out happily, for, although she detested her old-fashioned name, as a rule, she had learned, from long experience, that her father never addressed her in that way unless he was particularly gratified.

Mrs. Wallace adroitly arranged for the departure of her guests very soon after they arose from the table.

"Our friends think they cannot attend the masked ball with us this evening, dear," she observed to Mr. Wallace, "and, as we have promised to join the Heatherford party, I think we had better send them home first, then have the carriage return for us. No, no, Hetty; you must not urge Helen," she interposed, as Miss Wallace began to protest, and she gave her a significant glance at the same time. "She has already given you more than your share of her time, and her mother tells me that she wants her to herself this evening."

And so, shortly after seven, Helen and her mother were driven back to Mrs. Forsyth's.

The moment they reached their rooms, Mrs. Lancaster turned, and, to Helen's astonishment, caught her in her arms, and kissed her.

"My darling, I have some great news for you," she said almost breathlessly.

The fair girl flushed, then paled, with a conviction of what was coming.

"I—I suppose you saw Rob—Mr. Eggleston to-day," she faltered, with what calmness she could command.

"No, I didn't see Mr. Eggleston to-day," returned her mother, laughing, and mimicing the formal tone she had used. "Did you, dearie?" she added, searching her face curiously.

"Yes," said Helen wearily, and sinking into a chair, she put up her hands, to remove her hat, and to conceal the tears in her eyes.

"Did he see you, sweetheart?"

"Yes," and tears were in her voice now.

"Well—and didn't he appear to be glad to see you?"

"No—we—we did not recognize each other."

"And that was what made you dizzy and faint?" queried Mrs. Lancaster, sinking upon her knees beside the girl, and drawing her into her motherly arms.

Helen simply nodded—she could not speak—then dropped her head upon the friendly shoulder, with a heart-broken sob.

Mrs. Lancaster gave her a fond and vigorous hug; then a bright laugh rippled over her lips, and rang musically through the room.

The pretty brown head on her shoulder came up, with a jerk, and Helen stared at her mother in mingled amazement and indignation, great tears glittering on her lashes.

"Why, mamma!" she cried in a grieved, shocked tone.

But the shining eyes only smiled back into hers, and another light laugh parted the woman's red lips.

"Oh, you poor, deluded pair of lovers!" mocked the happy wife. "You have imagined that Rob's heart has been stolen from you, and Rob thinks that you are married, and lost to him forever."

"Oh! Did Rob hear that?" cried Helen, with a start. "Have you seen him?"

"No; I haven't seen him, as I said before; but I happen to know that he heard you were to marry somebody else on a certain day, and has been grieving his heart out ever since over your unfaithfulness to him."

"Mamma! Has he—truly?" cried Helen, her face lighting with an eagerness which proclaimed that she did not in the least sympathize with the heart-broken condition of the young man, but, rather, was elated by the fact. Then, attracted by her mother's dimpling cheeks and gleaming eyes, she added: "Mamma, what ails you? You are dealing in enigmas. You say you have not seen him. Who, then, has told you? How do you know?"

Her manner was eager—her tone quick and alert, very different from her previous depression and despair; for, if Rob still loved her, nothing else in the world mattered.

"What ails me, dearie? Why, nothing—only I believe I am the happiest being in the universe at this moment," said Margaret Lancaster, with that same triumphant ring in her tones that had attracted Helen at the Wallaces, "and you shall have the solution to my 'enigmas,' as you term them. It is true, I have not seen Rob, but I have seen some one who knows all about him, and who has told me how unhappy he has been ever since that misunderstanding arose between you and him, how unutterably wretched he was when he was told that you were to marry Hubert Alton."

Helen shivered slightly at having that terrible experience recalled, but her face softened with infinite tenderness as she thus learned of her lover's unswerving faithfulness to her.

"And—and he never cared for—Marjorie?" she questioned, with downcast eyes and flushed cheeks.

"No, dear; not the least little bit in the world; that was all a tale woven from Marjorie's fertile brain," was the grave reply.

"Who told you?" she demanded, sitting erect, her eyes now gleaming like stars.

"Mr.—Lancaster, Helen," said her mother, but blushing like a girl as she spoke the name.

Helen started violently.

"Mr. Lancaster!" she repeated, amazed. "Why, I thought——"

"Yes, dear," said the happy woman, as she again drew her into her arms, and laid her cheek against her shining hair. "I know of what you were thinking; I told you that he once did me a great wrong, and—and you inferred, from the way I related the story, that it was he who persecuted and annoyed me with his attentions, and caused the trouble between me and my husband, whom I left because he believed I was false to him——"

"Yes, I remember," said Helen in a tone of cold constraint as her companion paused, hardly knowing how to go on; "but I do not comprehend; you are still talking in enigmas," she went on, with a puzzled air. "You say that I inferred—I don't know what you mean."

"Helen, don't you remember anything disconnected or strange about my story? I told it so purposely, for I could not bear to have you know—the truth," faltered Mrs. Lancaster, for Helen's attitude was not encouraging. "My dear," with a sudden plunge, "Rob's uncle is—your father!"

CHAPTER XVIII.

"I CANNOT BELIEVE IT!"

For one awful moment after the foregoing paralyzing declaration, Helen sat staring blankly at her mother.

Then she sprang to her feet, with a half-stifled shriek.

"That man my father!" she cried wildly, and throwing out her hands, with a passionate gesture of repulsion. "Mamma, you cannot mean it! Oh, I cannot believe it! I will not believe it! I will not have it so!"

Mrs. Lancaster had also arisen, and now stood regarding the girl in blank dismay, mingled with wonder.

"Helen!" she said almost sternly, "I can understand that you are astonished at what I have told you, but I cannot understand such an unwarrantable display of passion and rebellion, in view of the fact. Perhaps I have done wrong to keep the truth from you for so many years. I fear I have made a grave mistake; but I did what I thought was for your best good. I felt sure, if I allowed you to know, during your childhood, that your father was living, your youthful curiosity would be aroused, and you would be continually asking questions that would be painful to me to answer. Indeed, I believed that he was the same as dead to me, and that we should never be reunited in this world. I knew, also, that, with your loving, sensitive temperament, you would ceaselessly yearn for him, and never be satisfied until you found him. I have said this to you already—when I recently revealed the fact that he was still living—and I will not rehearse. Going back still farther, you will remember how overcome I was when I learned, through that letter of Marjorie's to you, who Rob's uncle was. At first, I was so overcome that I thought the truth would have to come out. All the old bitterness was revived, however—yea, intensified, if that could be possible, for I had begun to realize that the proud and aristocratic uncle of your lover did not wish him to marry out of his own gilded circle, and when, like a thunderbolt, it was revealed to me that that uncle was my own husband, and your father, the blow seemed tenfold more crushing, and I said to myself that I would never allow you to marry Robert Eggleston. Of course, I had to give you some explanation, having betrayed so much, but I purposely made it blind, vowing to myself that you should never learn your real name, if I could help it. Even when we talked of this matter only a little while ago, although my feelings had begun to change somewhat, I could not bring myself to tell you that. I told you that, some time, I might reveal it, but I resolved to put off that day as long as possible, little dreaming it was so near. I think, Helen, that half that made me ill was fretting over the discovery that Mr. Lancaster was Rob's uncle, and the knowledge that, in spite of all my past suffering, I loved my husband still."

"Loved him! When he had insulted you in the worst possible way that a man could insult his wife!" interposed Helen in tones that rang with scorn.

"Yes, Helen; for, while I was ill, I began to realize that I had not been blameless. I should have been more patient—I should have waited until he had time to grow calm and reasonable, when he doubtless would have seen how he had wronged me," Mrs. Lancaster argued feelingly. "I had no right to leave him so summarily—without a word, making his home desolate, and dooming him to a terrible suspense. When I found that I was to become a mother, I felt, for a time, as if I had committed an unpardonable crime—as if I had stolen from him all the sweetest hopes of his life—and this sense of wrong grew upon me, and embittered my cup tenfold, after you came, for I knew you rightly belonged to him as much as to me. But I was proud and obstinate. I would not yield to take the first step toward a reconciliation. It was not until I began to fear that I was never going to recover from that illness, a year ago last winter, that I began to relent, and realize that Marien Ellsworth was more guilty than any one else—I have told you how she deliberately planned to ruin me, to gain the man whom she loved."

"Was it Mr. Lancaster whom she loved? I seem to be rather mixed regarding the two men," said Helen, somewhat sharply, as she recalled the fact that Mrs. Ellsworth and Marjorie had been in the same party with Mr. Lancaster and Rob during their travels.

"No; she loved the other."

"And who was the other?"

"My own cousin, John Wilton."

"Why, do you mean that Mr. Wilton who was at the Ellises, in the Adirondacks, two years ago?"

"Yes; although I did not know that he was in the place until the day before he left," said Mrs. Lancaster, with a sigh, as she recalled that painful interview. "He was the only child of my father's brother, and came to live with us when his own parents died. He was always fond of me, and was heart-broken when I chose another—but you know all that."

"Have you ever seen him since?"

"Yes. You remember the day that you went on the excursion, when you met Marjorie?"

"Yes."

"I went into the woods that morning to gather mosses. I took a book with me, and, while resting in the glen, John, who was out hunting, came suddenly upon me. I had not a suspicion until that moment that he was in the place. We had a harrowing interview, during which he expressed great sorrow for what he had done to mar my life; he even begged that he might settle a share of his wealth upon us, but I would not have allowed him to do so, even if we had not been beyond the need of it at that time. He mentioned that he had met you, and, a few days later, I heard you speak of having been introduced to a Mr. Wilton, some time previous, and you also stated that he had just left town."

"He was a nice-looking—a kind-looking—man, mamma. I remember that I was attracted to him," said Helen.

"He always was kind, and as generous as a prince, and my feelings have changed toward him, also of late; I hope I may meet him again some time, and tell him so," said her mother, a wistful look in her blue eyes. "I am so happy to-day, Helen, in view of this reunion with your father, I feel almost as if I could forgive my worst enemy," she concluded, with a tender thrill in her voice.

"Even Mrs. Ellsworth, perhaps?" said Helen bitterly.

"Poor woman!" said Mrs. Lancaster, with grave sweetness. I am sure that she must be very wretched, for no one can wrong others, as she has done, and maintain such a vindictive spirit as she has recently manifested, without bringing upon herself great suffering. Her sins must eventually recoil upon her own head."

"But, mamma, you have not yet told me how you happened to meet Mr.—Lancaster to-day," Helen observed, after a moment of silence.

Mrs. Lancaster told her of the accident in the grand stand, and which had so nearly proved to be of a serious nature, and how, just in the midst of it, Mr. Lancaster had suddenly appeared before her; how she had fainted, and he had afterward taken her to "The Antlers," where all the past had been explained and all sense of wrong and bitterness blotted out of their hearts.

"He feels very remorseful, Helen, because he has been working against his own child in opposing Rob's desire to marry you," she observed, after she had rehearsed the most important facts of the interview between herself and her husband.

"Oh! then he acknowledges having opposed it, does he?" said Helen, a crimson spot burning upon either cheek, while she wondered how much Mr. Lancaster had confessed to her mother.

"Yes; he admits that he took Rob away, hoping that he might get weaned from—well," and Mrs. Lancaster now flushed with embarrassment, "I may as well out with it—he could not be reconciled to the idea of his marrying the daughter of a common dressmaker."

"You were no 'common dressmaker,'" Helen sharply retorted, but secretly relieved, as she realized that her mother was still ignorant of the wretched and ignoble transaction between Mr. Lancaster and Hubert Alton.

"Well, but, dear, he did not know that."

"He might have known had he taken pains to inform himself," said Helen perversely. "It does not follow, because a woman is a dressmaker, a milliner, or follows some other trade, that she is 'common' or unfit to mate with her more fortunate fellow beings; there are doubtless thousands of women who have been tenderly reared and cultivated, and who have suddenly been reduced to poverty and the necessity of earning their daily bread. I have no patience or sympathy with such insufferable prejudice," the girl spiritedly concluded, her heart as hard as adamant against the man who had made use of such dishonorable measures to separate her from Rob.

"Helen," said her mother, regarding her in deep distress, "it is not like you to be so harsh and unforgiving. What has come over you, my child, to make you so bitter against any one, and especially against the father for whom you have always yearned?"

Helen flushed crimson under the reproof, turned sharply upon her mother, and opened her lips as if impelled to an angry retort; but she closed them resolutely again.

It had been upon the tip of her tongue to tell her about the letter and telegram, but something restrained her, and she merely returned in any icy tone:

"I think him worthy of all condemnation."

"But I love him, Helen—with all my heart and soul I love him, and—I have forgiven him," said Mrs. Lancaster, with quivering lips, a yearning tenderness in her tremulous lips.

Helen started and glanced into the pleading face before her. Her own softened instantly, and her conscience reproached her. She glided to her side and twined her arms lovingly about her.

"Have you, dear?" she queried gently. "Is there no lingering bitterness or regret in your heart?"

"No, my darling; only because of the fact that I did not forgive and become reconciled to him long ago," was the tearful reply. "You forget that I, also, have done wrong—that I, too, needed to be forgiven, and that he has suffered no less than I. Ah, Helen, I feel very humble, as well as joyful, in view of the great happiness that has come to me to-day."

"Then forgive me, mamma. I would not wound you for the world, and I will never utter another disparaging word in your presence again," Helen returned, as she kissed her tenderly.

"But that does not satisfy me, love," said her mother, searching her face, which had grown grave and sincere again. "I want you to receive him cordially, as your father—to take him into your heart and love him, as I do."

But Helen shrank from that as if she felt the sting of a lash.

Love that man who had bartered her like a piece of merchandise to keep her from marrying the man whom she adored?

She told herself that she never could—that she could never even take his hand in friendly greeting.

But, for her mother's sake, she felt that she must make an effort to repress all outward manifestation of this repugnance, and that she must reveal to her the secret of the letter and telegram.

Of course, she reasoned, Halburton Lancaster believed the matter was a secret to all the world save himself and Hubert Alton; he would never confess it, and she must never mar her idolized mother's newborn happiness by allowing her to even dream that he could be guilty of so dishonorable an act.

So she tried to smile as she evaded her last appeal by remarking:

"You must remember, mamma, that I have never known Mr. Lancaster personally. I have never even seen him, to know him, but once before to-day."

"And that was when you had that fall from your horse in Central Park?" interposed Mrs. Lancaster inquiringly.

"Who told you?" queried Helen in surprise.

"He himself; you never said anything about that accident to me, Helen."

"No; I was not in the least hurt, and I did not wish to have you worry about me when I was out riding.

I did not even know who the gentleman was at that time, but afterward, when we were speaking of the accident, Hubert Alton told me he was Mr. Lancaster, his employer," Helen explained.

"How strange it seems that his name was never mentioned in my presence until the day you received that letter from Marjorie!" said Mrs. Lancaster musingly. "But"— with a glance at the clock—"he is coming to me again to-night, to us, I should say—and he is going to bring Rob with him.

"Rob!" breathed the startled girl; but her tone was eager, her face grew tremulously tender, and a lovely blush crept up to her temples. "Ah!"—with an anxious gleam in her eyes—"what must he have thought of me to-day, mamma, when I passed him, looked straight into his eyes, and never made a sign to betray that I had ever known him!"

"It must have cut him keenly, dear, for he has never swerved a hair's breadth from his allegiance to you," said Mrs. Lancaster regretfully.

"Nor I to him, mamma," said Helen, with a sob; "but I was so paralyzed to see him there in the grand stand, when I did not dream that he was within hundreds of miles of us, that I simply could do nothing but stare at him."

"And he at you, for the same reason, perhaps," returned Mrs. Lancaster, with a silvery laugh, adding: "But you will soon make that right with each other."

But Helen's face had again settled into rigid lines, and there was a peculiar gleam in her great, brown eyes, for her thoughts had again reverted to that fatal letter and telegram.

"Shall I tell Rob about them?" she was asking herself; "shall I reveal to him how fearfully his uncle has wronged us both? He could never love or respect him afterward—he would learn to hate him as—as I do; yes, I do, in spite of all. Oh! shall I—shall I?"

"Helen! of what are you thinking?" demanded her mother, who had been silently watching her, and giving her a little shake to arouse her from her abstraction. "I have never, during all your life, seen such an unlovely look upon your face. Ah!"—in a tone of self-reproach—"can it be that, in my bitterness and pride and obstinacy of long ago, I tainted you with my own unforgiving and vindictive spirit, and it is now becoming apparent in your character? Heaven forbid, my darling, for it will poison your whole life if you do not conquer it, and I shall never forgive myself—never cease to reproach myself."

Helen looked up, shocked at her words.

"How unhappy I am making you, mamma," she exclaimed remorsefuly, "and it really does seem as if an evil spirit has taken possession of me to-day. But you must give me a little time to get used to—to the new régime," she concluded, with a sigh.

"Hark!" suddenly observed Mrs. Lancaster, with a start, as the bell in the hall below sounded through the house; "they have come! Helen, you will be kind to your father, for my sake, will you not? You will not make him feel that you cannot love him. Oh, he is a grand man, dear," she went on, with shining eyes and flushed cheeks. "One cannot look into his clear, true eyes or read his fine, sensitive face without knowing that he is good and noble through and through—and your eyes are very like his, Helen—you grow to look more like him every year."

A step was now heard coming up the stairs, and Helen began to quiver from head to foot.

"My dear, be calm! You must not get nervous; smooth your hair, and then we will go down," said her mother, but none too composed herself.

"Mamma, I can't—I can't see anybody but Rob tonight, and I cannot meet him in the presence of any one else," said the trembling girl wildly.

"But, Helen——" began her mother, growing pale.

"No—no; send Rob up to the little sitting-room across the hall, and I will go to him there," almost sobbed Helen, who was rapidly losing all control of herself.

"But, dearest," persisted Mrs. Lancaster, in a disappointed tone, "really, I——"

"I can't—I can't tell you," passionately interposed the girl, now shaking like a leaf, and, breaking from her mother's detaining arms, she dashed across the room and into her own chamber, shutting the door after her.

"Oh! he is a grand man! He is noble through and through!" she shrieked, under her breath, and with a hysterical laugh that rang mockingly through the room when she was alone.

The next moment she sank exhausted upon her bed, sobbing out in a weak and shaking voice:

"Rob! Rob! oh! Rob is true!—he loves me still."

CHAPTER XIX.

MR. LANCASTER ASTONISHES ROB.

As HELEN fled to the seclusion of her own room a servant knocked upon Mrs. Lancaster's door, and, upon being bidden to enter, presented her with a salver upon which rested four cards.

The woman's hand trembled visibly as she picked up the bits of pasteboard and read the names which she already knew were inscribed upon them.

"You can say to the gentlemen that I will be down immediately," she observed to the servant, who at once withdrew.

She then went to her dressing-case, where she gave a few touches to her hair and pinned a knot of blue ribbon among the folds of lace at her throat.

"He always liked me to wear blue," she murmured, and smiling happily into her own eyes.

She then unlocked a box that stood in the upper drawer and took from it a magnificent solitaire ring, which she slipped upon the third finger of her left hand, above the wedding-ring that she had always worn.

"I have never worn it since the dreadful day, but I never could part with it—not even when we were so poor, to save my life," she whispered, as she regarded the glittering stone with a fond look.

Then with an elasticity in her step that had long been strange to it, she went below to meet her husband and Rob.

Both gentlemen arose eagerly to greet her as she entered the parlor, although the younger man grew pale with disappointment and a sudden fear when he saw that she was alone.

Mr. Lancaster sprang to her side and gathered both her hands in his, while he searched her tender, smiling face, a luminous light upon his own.

"Rob," he said, turning to his nephew, "you have known this lady a long time, but I am inclined to think it becomes me to introduce her again to you to-night as my dear wife. Greet your aunt, my boy."

Rob needed no second bidding to prompt him to grasp the hand which she extended to him, or to bend and kiss the lips which she lifted for him to salute.

"I was always fond of Rob," said Mrs. Lancaster, with a quiver of deep feeling in her voice, "and"—giving his hand a stronger pressure—"I am glad to have you back again—how glad you cannot know."

"And Helen," faltered the young man, with another anxious glance toward the door.

Mrs. Lancaster flushed slightly.

"Helen said she was not equal to coming down with me," she replied, "but if you will go up-stairs to a small room opening off the landing to the right she will come to you there."

Rob's face lighted instantly, and, slipping from the room, he ran with nimble steps up to the second floor.

"Will Helen not come down to meet me?" queried Mr. Lancaster, as his nephew disappeared.

"Dear Hal, don't be troubled," said his wife tenderly, as she observed his grave expression; "she said she could not meet Rob in the presence of any one else."

"Ah, is that it?" queried the gentleman, with a smile of relief. Then, as he noted her trembling lips, he added: "Is that the only reason why she would not come down?"

And his wife, too ingenuous to deceive him, felt compelled to tell him something of the truth, although she made as light of the situation as possible.

"She cannot be quite reconciled to—to the past just yet," she said, "but I know she will soon get over that—she cannot fail to love you when she comes to know you."

"Just what do you mean by 'the past,' dear?" the man questioned, with paling lips.

"Oh, she thinks you—never should—have——"

"Doubted you, love?" he supplemented, as she faltered over the words.

"Yes, and—because she has felt that you depreciated her because of the business I have been obliged to follow," she added, with flushed cheeks.

"I have been an idiot!" he said, as he snatched her to him and kissed her passionately. "I am deeply humiliated for that folly."

"I can understand how you felt. You were as anxious to shield Rob from undesirable acquaintances as I have been to protect Helen in the same way," she said charitably. "Do not worry, dear; it will all come right in time."

But Mr. Lancaster was by no means reassured, and he found himself dreading the meeting with his daughter, with a sense of secret guilt that was almost unbearable.

While Rob is waiting with an anxious heart for Helen's appearance in the little sitting-room above, we will go back a few hours to the moment when Mr. Lancaster broke the news of the wonderful revelations of the day to him.

After leaving his wife at the Wallaces he drove directly back to the hotel, where, giving his team into the care of a groom, he sought his room.

He found Rob in the sitting-room adjoining, looking pale and wretched as he gazed from the window upon the moving crowds in the street, but apparently seeing nothing.

"Well, my boy," breezily observed the elder gentleman, "it was a fine show, wasn't it? I never saw anything to equal it before."

"Yes," responded Rob indifferently, but without looking up.

"I suppose you saw a certain little lady whom you used to know in the procession," said his uncle, thinking he might as well make a bold plunge. "She is prettier than ever, don't you think?"

What Rob thought was not distinguishable, for the sound he made was more like a groan than anything else, and his companion resolved that he would not keep him in suspense a moment longer."

"Now, Rob, I can't stand this sort of thing another minute," he remarked. "I know you have been perfectly wretched ever since you heard that the girl was married, and—so have I; even longer than that, for I am going to confess, here and now, that I planned to take you abroad with the hope that you would meet some one before our return who would—from a social point of view, at least—be a little better fitted to become your wife. I am ready now, however, to go down on my knees and beg pardon of you both—ready to make all possible restitution. But I will first relieve your mind by telling you that the girl you love is not married, as we supposed she——"

"Oh, Uncle Hal!" cried the young man, springing to his feet with the most remarkable revulsion of feeling. "Helen not married!—she is not Alton's wife?"

"No; something fortunately interposed almost at the last moment to save her from a fate that would have blighted her whole life as well as yours."

"Thank Heaven! But, really, the news seems too good to be true," said Rob, as he settled weakly back into the chair from which he had just arisen. "What happened to prevent the marriage?—ah, but she was to have been married to him," he interposed disconsolately, his face losing all its light again.

"Well, my boy, that can all be satisfactorily explained, and shall be later—she was simply driven to it by circumstances beyond her control," his uncle observed. "The match was broken off by the discovery of the man's total unworthiness; that also will have to be explained to you later, for I have another important piece of news that I must first confide to you, and that is—I have learned within the last hour and a half that she whom you have hitherto known as Helen Seymour is my own daughter."

Rob started erect again and stared blankly and anxiously at his uncle.

Surely such a statement as he had just made was almost sufficient to make him doubt his sanity.

But the man standing there before him with a proud and happy expression on his handsome face, with a tender, triumphant light in his dark eyes, such as he had never seen there before, convinced him that he was not only conscious of what he was talking about, but was filled with a deep and abiding joy because of his important assertion.

"But, Uncle Hal! I thought—I never heard that you had been married!" he said, when he could recover his breath.

"I know it, Rob, and I never meant you should know. But do you remember that when I refused my sanction to your engagement you asked me if I had ever loved?"

"Yes, and you seemed almost unmanned by the question; but I believed it was because you had been disappointed—that something had prevented you from marrying the woman whom you loved," the young man replied, but with his brain in a perfect whirl in view of what he had learned.

"No, Rob, I married the most beautiful—to me—

girl that ever lived—the woman whom you have known and so admired as Mrs. Seymour—and then, in a little more than a year, I so wronged and insulted her that—she went away and hid herself so effectually that I have never seen her since until today. But listen, and I will tell you all about it."

He seated himself opposite his companion and proceeded to give him a detailed account of what we already know, while Rob listened with constantly increasing wonder and joy in his heart as the remarkable story developed.

It was marvelous, he thought, that that glorious woman, whom he had so long revered, should prove to be his uncle's wife; and what a romance was unfolded to him!

Now he understood, as her perfidy was revealed, why he had always been repelled by Mrs. Ellsworth in spite of her kindness to him during their sojourn in Paris and her devotion to him when he was so ill at El Arish. Now she seemed, what she was, to him —utterly depraved.

He was a trifle troubled by his sense of obligation to her in spite of what he had learned, and mentioned the fact to Mr. Lancaster.

"Don't spend one moment of anxiety over that, Rob," said the man, with a gesture of repulsion, "for the woman has only been playing a deep game from the outset—everything she did was done with a set purpose in view: She meant to marry me and hoped to secure you for Marjorie. Forgive me, my boy," he continued regretfully, "that I ever allowed myself to be so deluded as to suggest such a thing to you, but I was blinded—I believe I was hypnotized, in fact."

"What opened your eyes to it? What makes you think that Mrs. Ellsworth was working for such a result?" Rob inquired, in surprise.

Mr. Lancaster did not at once reply—he seemed to be thinking deeply. At length he said:

"Well, under ordinary circumstances, I should shrink from telling any one of such an occurrence, but I am sure I can trust you not to mention it— the woman the same as proposed to me on the night of our arrival at Calcutta."

"But—but she knew that you were already married!" gasped Rob.

"No, she assumed that I had been divorced—and, if I had not been, I suppose she thought I could easily obtain a decree. But I soon convinced her that I had never had the slightest desire to be freed from the woman whom I still worshipped with all my heart, and for whom I had sought the world over. That was why she left the party so suddenly; she had risked all on one bold move, and, having lost, could not remain and face me during the remainder of the journey. I did not know then of what treachery she had been guilty in connection with my old trouble," the gentleman went on. "I have only learned that to-day, and words cannot express my contempt for the woman. I would like to be quits with her, though, for there is no doubt in my mind that her faithful nursing saved your life, let alone her motives. I think we will attend to that matter we talked over awhile ago; buy her a home—if Mrs. Sturdyvant thinks it will be as acceptable as anything—to save her from paying such a high rent, for, I suppose, she is having a pretty hard time of it."

"I should say she is reaping the just reward of her sowing," said Rob. "I have never heard of ingratitude like hers."

They discussed the situation and revelations of the day for awhile longer, and then, the gong sounding, went out to dinner, both men looking as if life had suddenly taken on a more attractive hue to them.

But Rob was so elated—the reaction from despair and grief to joy and hope had been so sudden that he could not eat. He simply dawdled over his food, while he asked a score of questions that kept his uncle busy answering.

All at once he put down his knife and fork and turned to Mr. Lancaster with a startled look.

"Uncle Hal, that makes Helen my cousin!" he said irrelevantly.

Mr. Lancaster smiled serenely.

"Don't be troubled about that, Rob," he said, as he calmly cracked a nut. "Your mother was simply my step-sister, although I was as fond of her as if the same blood had flowed in our veins. I have kept the fact from you because I wished you to feel that you really belonged to me."

"That was like your own generous-hearted self, Uncle Hal—you have been doing beautiful things all your life and never letting your right hand suspect what the left was about," said the young man gratefully, and with a sigh of relief over the question of consanguinity.

They were not to go to Mrs. Forsyth's until between eight and nine o'clock, and the delay taxed the young man's patience to the utmost limit. It seemed to him as if he could never realize the blessed news he had been told until he could hold Helen once more in his arms and hear from her own lips that she still loved him—that she had never wavered in her heart-allegiance to him.

Helen was free! He felt that he had never really known the meaning of that little word until now—she was free and would soon be his wife, for there was nothing now to hinder their early marriage.

He was thinking of this as he ascended the stairs at Mrs. Forsyth's and sought the little room on the right of the landing, where he had been told to wait for his dear one to come to him.

Presently a light step sounded in the hall; the next moment Helen entered the room and swung the door to after her.

She was all in white, just as he had seen her that afternoon, excepting the great black hat with its graceful plumes.

Her face was pale and still showed traces of the tempest that had so recently swayed her; but the love-light in her eyes assured him that her heart still beat steadfast and true for him.

He sprang forward with outstretched arms.

"My darling!" he whispered, too deeply moved to do more than that, and the next instant she was lying upon his breast, weeping from mingled joy and pain.

But joy was the stronger emotion, and the comfort of finding herself once more in Rob's arms, with the assurance that they would never be separated again, soon calmed her excited nerves and brought forth smiles to chase away the rain of tears.

Of course, when they were able to converse coherently, there was much to be talked over—the history of the last two years in connection with each to be related and discussed, and this took a long time.

Helen was amazed at what Rob told her regarding Marjorie's insinuations and reports about her, and of the fictitious stories she had pretended were in the letters she had written her, especially in connection with her contemplated marriage with Hubert Alton.

"I never wrote her one word upon the subject," Helen affirmed. "After she confessed to me her regard for you, hinted at your devoted attentions to her and her hope of winning you, I dropped all correspondence with her. It was not that I was jealous or cherished any ill will toward her; I was simply heartbroken because I believed that your love had been won from me, and I could not have the wound probed every now and then by having her love-affairs rehearsed to me."

"But how could she have known about the Alton affair—even to the very date and hour?" queried Rob, in perplexity. "She may have been corresponding with Alton himself, for aught I know," he added. "I could believe almost anything of her in that line of deception if she could pretend to read what she did apparently from an old letter of yours—for it certainly was your handwriting."

"She may have heard your uncle mention the fact," suggested Helen, as she remembered the correspondence that had passed between Mr. Lancaster and Hubert Alton, and the fact of Marjorie's intimacy with the former; "you know that Mr. Alton was a clerk in his employ."

"Perhaps," Rob assented, "but Uncle Hal never breathed a word of it to me if he knew it. I suppose, however, he would not, knowing what he did of our previous relations. But, Helen, why do you speak of him so distantly as 'your uncle'? Why do you not say 'my father'?" and he searched her face earnestly, as he put the questions.

She flushed hotly beneath his gaze.

"It seems so new—so strange," she faltered.

"And you have not seen him yet! How selfish of me to keep you here so long," the young man added remorsefully. "Come! come down with me now to greet him."

But the fair girl shrank visibly at the suggestion.

"No—I cannot, Rob—at least, not to-night," she replied, with an unmistakable shiver.

"Helen, dear, I am afraid you are not feeling quite right toward Uncle Hal," said her lover gravely. "You still feel aggrieved over his old distrust of your mother—is it not so?"

"And, oh, Rob! he tried his best to separate you and me!" she burst forth passionately.

"I know—he confessed to me this afternoon that he hoped, by taking me abroad, to wean me from you; but he is truly sorry now and is ready to make all possible restitution," her lover returned. "Cannot you forgive him, Helen?" he pleaded earnestly.

"Oh! shall I tell him?" queried the girl to herself, as she pressed her hands upon her breast, where she had concealed those two fatal papers until she could decide what final disposition to make of them; for it had occurred to her that if her mother should happen to go to her desk for anything and discover them her peace of mind would be destroyed.

But something held her back from disclosing the secret to Rob—something seemed to tell her that it would be weak and cowardly to destroy the young man's love and respect for him who had been both father and mother to him—who had been his ideal par excellence.

Rob was grieved by her silence, little dreaming of the terrible struggle that she was having with her self.

"Uncle Hal is a noble man, dearest," he continued, after awhile, "one of the noblest I have ever known. I do not claim that he may not have made mistakes during his life— who does not?—but I am sure that he has made fewer than most men."

Then he went on to relate instances of how the man, with his great, generous heart, had relieved the poor, lifted up the fallen, and thrown himself into many a breach to prevent foul wrongs in both public and private life.

Helen listened quietly to it all, but when he begged her again to go down with him she shrank as before.

"I cannot to-night, Rob—indeed, I cannot," she said again and he did not urge her further.

CHAPTER XX.

WEDDING BELLS.

It was after eleven o'clock when Mr. Lancaster finally took leave of his wife to return to his hotel.

"I will not disturb Rob," he said, with a regretful sigh over having to go without seeing Helen, "let him make the most of this reunion; but to-morrow, dearest, I shall insist upon having my family all together—that is, if I can possibly arrange for it, which may be somewhat difficult, as the city is so full during carnival week. At all events, I shall come to you again early—say about ten."

Half-an-hour later Rob bade Helen good night, he also promising to come early the following morning.

There were four very happy people in Colorado Springs that night, and yet Mr. Lancaster was kept awake far into the "wee sma'" hours, from a feeling of anxiety and foreboding because of the attitude that Helen had assumed toward him.

Before he slept, however, he had resolved to have a full understanding with her at the earliest opportunity; their future relations must be definitely established, be they for or against him.

It was only a few minutes after nine the next morning when a servant sought Helen, who was in her mother's room writing a note to Hetty Wallace.

She had promised to lunch with Hetty that day, and she was explaining why she could not keep her appointment.

"There is a gentleman in the parlor to see you, Miss Seymour," the servant informed her, adding;

"and he said please excuse him for neglecting to send up a card, as he neglected to bring any with him."

Helen's face was luminous as she put aside her writing and arose with alacrity to go below.

She, of course, expected that Rob had come early, as he had promised, although she had not looked for him before ten.

As she entered the parlor a tall, distinguished-looking man, with snow-white hair, arose to greet her, and a low, half-stifled cry escaped Helen as she instantly recognized Mr. Lancaster.

In spite of her antagonism against him and her chagrin at being thus taken by surprise, she could but acknowledge that he was a most noble specimen of manhood.

His clear brown eyes looked kindly and yearningly into hers as he drew near her, and she was at once impressed that they were very like her own—as was also the shape of his brow—and she was thrilled, in spite of herself, by their magnetic glance.

"My dear," he began entreatingly, "I have to ask your pardon for coming to you so early, but I could not rest until I had seen you. I have come to plead for forgiveness and love of my child. Your mother has accorded me hers, Rob also; and even though I can never forgive myself, or cease to regret the mistake I have made, I beg that you, too, will be generous and open your heart to me. Ah! if you could know how, all my life, I have yearned to have a daughter at my fireside and to brighten my home!"

Helen had stood with downcast eyes and compressed lips while he was speaking. She felt like bursting into wildest weeping; but her pride rebelled against breaking down in any such weak way before him.

She was very lovely, her companion thought, as his eyes dwelt fondly upon her. She had on a dress

LOVE'S CONQUEST

of delicate pink chambrey trimmed with ruffles of the same edged with white braid, and the color was very becoming to her pure complexion, and contrasted beautifully with her dark hair and eyes.

Her fair, slender hands were clasped before her, and Mr. Lancaster, quick to take in every detail, observed that on the third finger of her left hand there gleamed a pure white stone, which he felt confident was the "souvenir of friendship" of which Mrs. Lancaster had told him, that Rob must have replaced there.

"Helen, my child——" he pleaded, as she did not —could not, in fact—speak; and he went a step nearer to her.

She lifted her eyes to his, searched his face for one brief moment, then turned abruptly away from him with a despairing gesture, and walked to the window.

There was a terrible struggle going on within her as she stood there, looking out upon the street with clouded eyes, while the man behind her watched her, his brows contracted with pain.

Presently she slipped one hand within the folds of her dress, and the next instant turned back to her companion, holding out two folded papers to him, her face white as alabaster.

"Can I—could any one forgive—these?" she questioned, in a scarcely audible voice, but without meeting his glance.

The man took them mechanically, cold chills chasing rapidly over his body at the sight of them.

As he unfolded them a groan of anguish burst from him, as he realized that the secret he had devoutly hoped would never be unearthed was known to her.

"No," he said, after a moment, but speaking with difficulty, "I have no right to ask you to pardon this

—I see that you know the extent of my wrong—the depths to which I have fallen."

He was silent again for a minute, while he ran his eye swiftly through the letter and message, a feeling of unutterable contempt for himself surging through his heart.

Then he suddenly, almost spasmodically, crumpled the papers in his hand.

"Will you tell me how you came by them?" he queried huskily. "Did he—Alton—give them to you?"

"No," Helen replied, while something of pity stirred within her for the anguish which she saw written upon his face, "the girl whom he had wronged brought them to me; they came into her possession by accident, and, in her despair upon learning what he was intending to do, she came to beg that I would not make her wrong irreparable. What she told me of herself was sufficient to make me realize that I had been saved from a fate that would have been unendurable even had she not presented these proofs of a plot to ruin my whole life."

An involuntary groan burst from Halburton Lancaster.

"May I keep them?" he asked, yet hardly knowing what he said in his deep humiliation.

"Certainly; I have no further use for them," and there was a ring of scorn in the fair girl's tone that cut the man like the keen edge of a knife.

He turned away from her with a despairing gesture, sank into a chair, and bowed his head upon his hands.

Helen stood irresolute. She had not been quite prepared for remorse like this; she had expected he would offer excuses, argue the point, and try to exonerate himself.

Instead, he appeared to accept her judgment and scorn of him as well merited and beyond all pardon.

Presently she moved softly toward the door. She did not know what else to do. She could not tell him that she forgave him, and she could not remain there to witness his suffering.

Mr. Lancaster suddenly lifted his head.

"One moment, please," he said, in a hollow tone; "does—does your mother know of this?"

Helen turned back and drew nearer to him.

"No, I have never told mamma," she said, "I could not when it first happened because it caused her such pain to speak of you; and—and something has always seemed to restrain me since, whenever I thought of doing so. I do not think I can ever tell her now, for—I would not mar her recovered happiness for anything."

"Thank you," said Mr. Lancaster gratefully; then added huskily, "and—and Rob?"

"Rob shall never know from me," returned Helen coldly.

The wording of the sentence, or perhaps it was the slight emphasis, stung the proud man to his very soul.

He started to his feet, and Helen saw that his face was as white as the hair that crowned his grandly shaped head.

"I will tell them both," he asserted passionately. "I deserve to be humiliated to that extent. I don't know what ever made me do such a thing," he went on, in a hopeless tone. "I think I was tempted of the devil, and I have never known a peaceful moment since the vile scheme took form in my brain. I admit that I deserve neither your love nor respect, Helen, though there is nothing I would not do to atone for my sin, if I might but hope to attain them in time. I will confess the whole affair to your mother and Rob before the day is over, even though they also banish me from their affections forever."

Actuated by some impulse which she could not control, Helen glided to his side and laid her hand upon his arm.

"No, you must not do that," she said, in a tone of quiet authority. "I will not have my mother's present happiness marred by a single shadow, for I love her far too well and she has seen sorrow enough. As for Rob, I know you are as dear to him as my mother is to me, and I am unwilling that any barrier should come between you, through any act of mine. I could not be a hypocrite, though," she went on, flushing.

"I had those papers, I knew what they meant, and it seemed the only honest, straightforward thing for me to do, to give you the true reason for——"

"I understand you, Helen," said the man gravely, as she paused for a suitable word. "You are a noble girl, and I believe I fully appreciate your position. For myself, I have arrived at a point where I would stop at nothing in the way of atonement for what I have done; but, as you imply, I am not the only one to be considered—your mother and Rob would also suffer keenly if they should learn the truth. How true it is that one cannot fall without dragging others down with him! It is noble in you to wish to spare them and so, in mercy, spare me, too. I am grateful to you for your forbearance," he concluded, with a thrill in his voice that touched her deeply.

Their eyes met—those two pairs of eyes that were so alike in color, expression, and shape—and the girl was startled at the whirl of thoughts that went seething through her brain.

"Am I noble, as he says?" she asked herself. "If so, may it not be possible that I partake somewhat of his nature, since he is my father? Rob says he has led a noble life—that he is always doing good to others. I know of but two instances during his whole career to offset a lifetime of goodness. Have I a right to condemn him utterly—to cherish hatred in my heart against him for those two mistakes? Hatred! What an ugly word it is! Can it be true, as mamma said, that I have been tainted with the pride, obstinacy, and vindictiveness which she manifested so long ago? My mother, whom I have looked upon as perfection personified—and that they will poison my whole life if I do not conquer them? Can I marry Rob and be happy while secretly hating the one whom he loves as a father—to whom he owes all that he is? No really ignoble man could have reared him to be the true-hearted man that he is. It was his mistaken pride and love for Rob that tempted him to do wrong, and now, having learned that it was against his own child that he has sinned, his punishment is surely very bitter. Oh! what am I? Am I infallible that I should judge him, or any one, to the point of hating?" and tears started to her eyes as she thus analyzed the situation and began to realize her own weaknesses.

Her companion had watched her narrowly, and was convinced from the varying expressions of her face that a conflict was going on within her, and when he caught sight of the tears in her eyes his sore heart was a trifle comforted.

But he wisely concluded to drop the subject under discussion for a time, and he broke the silence that was becoming awkward by observing:

"I have arranged for us all to be together as a family—have secured pleasant apartments at 'The Antlers,' where we will remain until we can decide where we would like to reside permanently. What do you think will be the best for your mother, Helen—to remain in the West for the present, or would she prefer to return to New York?"

"I have wished that mamma might live here for another year," thoughtfully replied the girl, "for, although she seems to be perfectly well now, there are times when I notice an inclination to cough. We were intending to go back to New York next month, for our means are limited, and she felt that she must resume business again, while I was intending to teach."

"Of course there will be no necessity for anything of that kind now," said Mr. Lancaster, in a tone of decision. "I have abundant resources, and henceforth neither of you is to know a care or have a wish ungratified. I think, myself, it would perhaps be wise to spend a year or two longer here. Do you like the place, Helen?"

"I think it beautiful—grand!" she responded, her face kindling as her eyes roved out over the mountains, which could be seen from the window, "and the climate is delightful—there have been but very few days that we have not seen the sun during our sojourn here; we have no long storms or cold east winds such as we have at home."

Mr. Lancaster smiled. He could see that she, at least, would not be averse to remaining in that land of almost perpetual sunshine.

"Will it be agreeable to you to go to 'The Antlers' for awhile?" he inquired.

"Certainly," Helen replied; for, of course, wherever her mother and Rob were to be there she could be content.

At that moment Rob himself entered the gate, and, espying her through the window, nodded a smiling greeting and then came directly in without the ceremony of ringing.

He looked gratified upon finding Helen and his uncle together, although he made no comment upon the fact, and Mr. Lancaster, glancing at his watch, observed that a double carriage would be at the door in just fifteen minutes, and asked Helen if she would inform her mother, so that she might be ready to accompany them upon a drive.

Rob and Mr. Lancaster had already had a confidential talk that morning, during which the gentleman had informed his nephew that he was at liberty to settle himself in life whenever and wherever he chose, and he would see that he was well established in any business that was most congenial to him.

That same evening Helen and Rob freely discussed the subject, and decided that they would be married about the middle of the following month and locate in Colorado Springs for the present, Rob thinking that he would like to study mining—that business appearing to him to offer flattering prospects for the future.

This decision met with the approval of both Mr. and Mrs. Lancaster, who at once set about making preparations for the important event.

The former purchased a handsome house that was just being completed on one of the fine avenues of the city, and had a deed of the property made out in Helen's name.

Then he and his wife proceeded to furnish it, on the quiet, for it was to be a wedding-gift and a complete surprise to the young couple on the day of their marriage.

Mrs. Lancaster was also very busy superintending the making of the trousseau for the bride-elect, as she would not trust any one's taste but her own, although her husband insisted that she should order largely from New York such articles as could be purchased ready-made.

The wedding had been set for the fifteenth of September, and was to take place in Grace Church exactly at noon.

Hetty Wallace had been asked to serve as "maid of honor," and a friend of hers was to officiate as "best man" for Rob; while the ceremony was to be followed by a wedding-reception and elegant breakfast at "The Antlers."

The young people thought, at first, that they would not care for a tour, but Mr. Lancaster said that urgent business was calling him to New York, and, as he could not think of leaving his wife behind, and knew that Helen would keenly feel a separation from her mother, he suggested that they all make the trip together, returning late in October, when they would all settle down quietly for the winter.

This plan was unanimously adopted, and Helen actually found herself looking forward to a visit among some of her old school friends—upon the Benyons in particular, although she still avoided her father's society when she could do so without attracting the notice of others.

The wedding-morning dawned bright and cloudless, and a little before noon a small but brilliant company gathered in the pretty stone church to witness the ceremony that was to unite, for life, the hands and loving hearts of our two loyal lovers.

For the sake of Rob and her mother, as well as to prevent all gossip, Helen had made no protest when, as a matter of course, it was planned that Mr. Lancaster should give her away; and when the hour arrived and she passed down the aisle, leaning on his arm, to the altar, where Rob was awaiting her, she involuntarily drew a deep breath of delight at the sight that met her eyes, for the church had been transformed into a fairy bower of wondrous beauty.

White chrysanthemums and feathery asparagus vine—in which Mr. Lancaster had seen her embowered on the day of the carnival—had been chosen to decorate the place. The whole aisle, clear to the chancel, had been arched with these flowers and foliage. The chancel had also been banked on three sides with green and white, and another arch placed just before the altar, and underneath which the couple were to plight their vows. This was surmounted by two clasped hands, wrought in white immortelles on a bed of green, and just below was a monogram composed of the letters E and L.

The bride wore white Lyons satin, the corsage embroidered with pearls, and otherwise decorated with costly lace.

The veil was of simple tulle, fine and fleecy as a cobweb, and she carried a magnificent cluster of bride-roses without foliage.

Miss Wallace was attired in finest of mousseline de soie over white silk, with simply a great handful of maiden-hair ferns to break the dead white of her costume.

The ceremony was made very impressive by the clergyman, who had been exceedingly kind to Mrs. Lancaster and Helen when the clouds had hung darkest over them; he had stood by them, stanch and true, and the fee which Mr. Lancaster had insisted should be given him was substantial enough to testify to the appreciation of all those most interested.

It was a lovely wedding, and the breakfast was in keeping with everything else, and when it was over and the guests gone, Mrs. Lancaster observed to Rob and Helen:

"We have a little surprise awaiting you, my children, and a carriage is at the door ready to take us for a short drive."

"But, mamma, I cannot go out like this," Helen replied, glancing down at her dress.

Instead of replying, Mrs. Lancaster removed the veil from her head and threw a spotless opera-cloak over her costume, whereupon Mr. Lancaster told the young husband and wife that they were to follow him and ask no questions.

CHAPTER XXI.

"SHE HAS FOGIVEN ME!"

THE bride and groom, looking somewhat perplexed, followed the elder people from the room, entered the closed carriage that was waiting at the door, and were driven away amid showers of flowers that were thrown at them by the guests of the house with whom they had made friends.

Mr. and Mrs. Lancaster kept up a lively conversation during the drive, to prevent questions, and at last they stopped before the handsome residence that had been prepared for the young couple, and where a number of their friends had gathered to welcome them.

"Rob, what is the meaning of all this?" queried Helen, as they were following Mr. and Mrs. Lancaster into the house.

"I haven't the slightest idea," said the young man, looking greatly mystified.

They entered the reception-hall, which had been beautifully furnished and decorated, and here, amid much laughter and jollity, they were bidden "Welcome home."

Then it dawned upon Helen that this was the "surprise" of which her mother had spoken, and it also accounted for the many mysterious trips which the elder couple had made by themselves during the last two or three weeks.

The whole party went through the house together and found it complete in every department, the furnishings comprising the nicest of everything; and, after this pleasant supplement to the wedding, their friends took their departure, with many congratulations and good wishes for the young people's future.

When Helen went to her dressing-room to exchange her bridal attire for a pretty home gown, her entire wardrobe having been transferred from the hotel to her home during her absence at the church, she found, lying conspicuous upon her toilet-table, a legal-looking envelope addressed to Mrs. Robert Eggleston.

On opening it she found the deed of gift which made over to her that beautiful home and all that it contained, and signed by both her father and mother.

"A 'surprise,' indeed," she murmured, with tremulous lips, but with clouded eyes, for she was conscious that she was not in just the right frame of mind to accept such a generous gift from her father.

When she went below she found Mr. and Mrs. Lancaster waiting to take leave of her, their carriage having remained to take them back to the hotel.

"Mamma! you are not going away!" exclaimed Helen, with a note of protest in her tones.

"Yes, dear; your father and I are going for a little trip to Cripple Creek; we leave early to-morrow morning. Meantime, you and Rob are to enjoy your home to the utmost," Mrs. Lancaster responded, adding: "You will find everything complete, I think, even to a couple of well-trained servants. We shall return on Saturday evening, and then on Monday, you know, we all start for New York. I hope you are pleased with the house, Helen."

"How could I help it, mamma? it is perfectly lovely," replied the young bride, with starting tears, as she kissed her mother fondly. Then she turned to Mr. Lancaster and put out her hand to him. "Thank you—thank you for what I found on my table up-stairs; but I feel that I do not quite deserve it," she tremulously observed.

He drew her into his arms and folded her in a close embrace.

"My darling, be happy, that is all I ask," he murmured, and then, unable to say more, he left her abruptly and conducted his wife to the carriage.

The next few days were like a beautiful dream to Helen and her husband, who seemed like a pair of happy children in their lovely home.

It was simply perfect in all its appointments, and as Mrs. Lancaster had secured an efficient woman to act as housekeeper together with a younger servant to assist her, Helen found that she had absolutely no care and was free to be as happy as she chose.

They found a pair of bays and a handsome carriage in the stable in the rear of their dwelling, and the pretty monogram composed of the letters E. and L. on various plates and panels plainly indicated for whom the equipage had been provided, and the young couple spent much of their time in driving.

They were at the station on Saturday evening to meet Mr. and Mrs. Lancaster, who cordially accepted their invitation to come home with them, and the four spent a quiet, restful Sabbath together.

Monday evening they all left for the East, the house being given over to the care of Mrs. Mathews, the housekeeper, during their absence.

Upon their arrival in New York, the Waldorf-Astoria became their temporary abiding-place, whence they sent cards to the friends whom they were desirous to meet.

Helen's and her mother's first visit was made to Mary Wadleigh, who was still keeping house for "Mr. Smith" in the small suite which they had formerly occupied.

The girl was overjoyed to see them, her face

beamed with happiness as she welcomed and led them into the pretty parlor, which was as bright and neat as a new pin.

"Oh, Mrs. Seymour and Miss Helen, I cannot begin to tell you how happy I am, for, will you believe it? I was married to Hubert a week ago last Wednesday," she cried, as she wiped the glad tears from her cheek.

"Why, mamma!" exclaimed Helen astonished at the strange coincidence, for that had been her own wedding-day

"It is singular, dear," Mrs. Lancaster returned. Then addressing Mary again, she remarked: "You must tell us how the baby is, and then we shall want to hear about the important event."

"Oh, Katherine—we have called her that for my mother—is well and getting to be a great girl, and she was christened on the day that we were married. Hubert is really getting to be very fond of her, too," said Mary, with shining eyes. "Mr. Smith was the one who brought it about," she went on, in a grateful tone; "he has been as kind as a father to me. He had not been here long before he got my whole story, and then, right away, although I did not dream of any such thing, he began to make friends with Hubert, without letting him suspect his object, at least until he gained his confidence, and made him think there was no one in the world like him. Of course Hubert never came here, so he did not know that Mr. Smith knew anything special about him or his history. When he finally told him that he knew all my story, Hubert was at first inclined to be obstinate and resentful; but there came a day when he owned up, like a man, that he had done me a great wrong and was willing to make all the reparation in his power. Mr. Smith didn't give him any time to change his mind, but arranged at once for a quiet wedding here, and made us some very handsome and useful presents to give us a start. The man is always hunting around for some one to be good to; he has hired the suite opposite this and fitted it up beautifully to make a home for eight poor girls, who were not able to earn enough to pay their way. I take care of them and supply their table, they paying just enough to cover expenses, while I get a nice little sum for what I do. Hubert told me yesterday that I need not do the work any longer, for his salary is sufficient to support us; but I am fond of the girls and I like it. Hubert, Mr. Smith, and I occupy this apartment by ourselves now, and we are really very happy."

"This is truly welcome news," said Mrs. Lancaster, in a tone of hearty sympathy, "and I am sure the gentleman has shown himself a good friend to you."

"Indeed he has, and to others as well," warmly returned Mary. "He is in the city most of the time now, for he is going to build a large home for poor girls; the foundation is already laid. He says that I may be matron of it, if I like, when it is done. I told him I thought I was too young, but he says I have managed so nicely here, and really seem older than I am, he thinks I would make a good one. I haven't quite made up my mind, but I'm inclined to take the position, for I believe that such girls should have some one over them who can sympathize with them in their hardships and give them a helping word now and then," she concluded, with a great dignity and womanliness which indicated that she had developed greatly in character during the last year.

Yes, she had heard from her father, she said in reply to Mrs. Lancaster's inquiry. She had written him all about herself as soon as she was married, and he had replied at once, saying that she was freely forgiven all the past, that he had been ill for several months and very anxious about her. He invited her to come home whenever she liked, to bring her husband with her, and let the past be forgotten.

"We are going to Boston next Saturday, to make our visit, and my heart is full of joy, in spite of the sorrow and regret from which I never expected to be fully free," she observed, with emotion. "And, Miss Helen," she went on, turning to her with tearful eyes, "if it had not been for your exceeding kindness, I believe I should never have been where I am to-day; I shall love you and your mother as long as I live."

Mrs. Lancaster and Helen then told her something of their own experiences since leaving New York, and Mary was both astonished and delighted over the romance of their story and their flattering prospects for the future.

They sat chatting with her for more than an hour, admired and petted Katherine, when she woke from her nap, and who was really a beautiful and interesting child.

Then Mary showed them over the other suite, which was truly a very pretty and homelike place for those whom it was intended to benefit, and both Mrs. Lancaster and Helen experienced a deep admiration for and interest in the gentleman who was doing so much good for others.

Then they went back to the other apartment, for they had left their wraps in Mary's parlor, and while they were standing in the hall exchanging a few last words, a latchkey was inserted in the lock of the outer door, and the next moment "Mr. Smith" stood before them.

He glanced in surprise at the strangers, then he suddenly lost every atom of color.

"Margaret!" he faltered, as his glance met the eyes of the astonished woman.

"John!" she involuntarily exclaimed; then, after a

moment of hesitation, took a step forward and held out her hand to him.

He took it mechanically, but seemed unable to utter a word, and she, with her quick woman's wit and to cover his confusion, exclaimed:

"Well, I am surprised! Mary," turning to the young woman, who was regarding them with wondering eyes, "your 'good Mr. Smith' proves to be my own cousin, John Smith Wilton, and it seems that he has been hiding both himself and his generous deeds under his very common middle name. Helen, you remember Mr. Wilton? You met him in the Adirondacks two summers ago."

And Helen, following her mother's example cordially greeted the man, realizing that he was the cousin who had played such a conspicuous part in that sad drama of her early life.

"Now, John, Helen and I thought we had some errands that must be attended to; but they can wait," Mrs. Lancaster continued. "Come with us into the parlor, for I have some things that I wish to say to you. I am sure Mary will excuse us, for we have not seen each other for so long."

The man followed her in silence, wondering at her happy, care-free face, more lovely than ever it seemed to him, and at her elegant costume; but most of all at the wonderful change in her manner toward himself.

"So you are the Mr. Smith' who hired our suite through Mr. Benyon!" continued Mrs Lancaster, as soon as they were by themselves and whose thoughts had been very busy ever since her cousin's unexpected appearance. "Did you know whom you were helping out of serious difficulties when you agreed to take it?"

"Y-es, Margaret."

"Perhaps," she went on, flushing and bending a searching look upon him, as another startling thought flashed through her brain, "you also know something about that other transaction. Were you also the purchaser of our cottage in the Adirondacks? I always thought that a remarkably quick and profitable sale —do you?"

"Ah!" as his eyes wavered and he moved uneasily in his chair, "I am answered. You are the present owner of that cottage, are you not, John?"

"But I could not bear to know that you were suffering, Margaret," said the man, in a tone of humble apology, as if he had been detected in some crime.

There were tears in the beautiful woman's eyes as they rested gratefully upon him.

"How did you know that we were suffering, John? How did you happen to discover the fact so opportunely?" she softly questioned, for she was deeply moved.

"Well, since you have found me out, you may as well have the whole story," said Mr. Wilton, with a laugh of embarrassment. "I was in Mr. Benyon's library, which adjoins the reception-room, the afternoon that your daughter, called and confided to him the trouble you were in, and of course I heard all that was said. Perhaps——"

"And so you seized the opportunity to pour some of your wealth, which I had rejected the year before, into my unwilling hands. You have not only given me back my life and health, but inexpressible happiness as well," interposed Mrs. Lancaster, with emotion. "I should have died if we had not secured that much needed money just at that time; and then—and then—— Oh, John! I owe you more than you can dream of!"

She broke down utterly here, buried her face in her handkerchief, and cried softly for several minutes.

John Wilton regarded her with increasing wonder, but presently he observed huskily:

"I do not think I quite understand you, Margaret."

She lifted her head and dashed the tears from her cheeks. Then, springing to her feet, she approached him with both hands extended.

"Oh, you good, generous-hearted fellow! you shall understand," she said, with tremulous lips, "and I need to ask your forgiveness, for I have wronged you deeply. I have been proud, selfish, and unkind; I have thought only of myself, and never paused to consider that others were the victims of circumstances as well as myself, and that I was increasing their sufferings through my mistake and wilfulness——"

"Margaret, what has changed you so? To what do I owe this return of friendliness and kindness?" interposed her cousin, as he held her hand in his trembling grasp and searched her face with eager eyes.

"When one goes down deep into the 'valley of the shadow,' one sees one's own life from a different standpoint," she huskily returned. "Only a little more than a year ago, John, I thought the end had come for me, and I began to realize what sad mistakes I had made and to feel more kindly toward some whom I had once said I would never forgive—yourself among the number——"

"Do you mean it, Margaret?" cried the man, a great joy quivering through his tones; "can you at least forgive me for my mad and selfish love for you, for allowing myself to be hoodwinked by a base woman into insulting you as I did? I might have known, if I had stopped to reason, that you would never be disloyal to the vows you had taken, that you would never encourage me or consent to receive me privately, as was represented to me that you wished to do. I have never ceased to lament my folly nor to yearn for your pardon."

"It is yours, John; I freely put all the past behind me, and sincerely regret the spirit I manifested when we met two years ago," said Mrs. Lancaster, with a sigh. "Your noble work for the unfortunate, the good you have accomplished in this house, for the poor girl whom we tried to benefit, together with your delicate and generous provision for us when we were in such sore need, have shown me that I have misjudged you. Besides," smiles beginning to dimple her cheeks, "happiness is a great leveler of all differences, and I am now very, very happy, John."

"Margaret! do you mean that you have found—your ——" began John Wilton, with trembling lips.

"Yes, Hal and I have at last found and become reconciled to each other, after all these years," she said, with shining eyes that told their own story. "You must come to see us, John—we are are at the Waldorf—and be friends again with him. He knows all the truth now; he never knew of Marien's agency in that dreadful affair until I told him recently, and he will be glad to show you that he realizes that he was rash and unjust, as well as I."

"Will he?" queried John Wilton gravely, and Margaret could feel that he was trembling from head to foot, for he still held her hands.

"Ah!" she said deprecatingly. "I remember what hard things he said to you that day, but—but, suppose you had been in his place, John? Perhaps he will take the first step; perhaps he will come to you, if you will receive him," she pleaded. "I am so happy myself I want all the world to be happy and at peace also," she concluded, with a yearning sigh.

The man before her bent and reverently touched the hands he was holding, then released them, and as he did so there shone upon his face a look of lofty self-renunciation that almost made Helen, who had been a deeply moved witness of the foregoing scene, weep.

"Margaret, to see you happy once more, to see this

look upon your face that you wore as a girl, is a boon that I would long ago have given my dearest earthly hopes to achieve," he said smiling frankly into her uplifted eyes, even though he was very white about the mouth. "I will come to the Waldorf to see you," he added, "to-morrow, perhaps, if that will be agreeable to you."

"Thank you, John, thank you; yes, come," Margaret responded, but with a sob in her throat, for something in his face and voice made her heart ache.

Mr. Wilton then turned from her to Helen, whom he began to fear he was neglecting.

"I remember you well, Miss Helen—Miss Lancaster, I suppose I must call you now. We met at Mrs. Sturdyvant's in the Adirondacks; but I did not dream that you were the daughter of one who had been very dear to me from childhood," he observed, his eyes lingering upon her lovely face.

"I have not forgotten you, Mr. Wilton," Helen began, and would have said more, but her mother laughed out musically and checked her.

"Helen," she said, "we must not allow you to be 'missed' any more to-day. John, my daughter became Mrs. Robert Eggleston a week ago last Wednesday, and whom do you suppose the young man is?"

"I haven't the slightest idea," said Mr. Wilton, smiling at the young bride's blushes.

"Well, she met and became fond of him years ago, when they were in the high school together, and—he has turned out to be Hal's nephew, whom he has reared as a son," Mrs. Lancaster explained.

"How wonderful!" exclaimed her listener.

"Isn't it?—and romantic, too! But we really must go now. Come to-morrow, early in the afternoon, and you shall have the whole story in detail," said Margaret, moving toward the door.

John Wilton went down to the street with them,

assisted them into their carriage, and watched them drive away, the fair woman whom he had loved from his boyhood, looking back and smiling a friendly adieu to him as the vehicle turned the corner.

Then he went back to the little parlor and stood with bowed head upon the spot where she had held out her hands to him.

How long he would have remained there no one can say had he not been aroused by the ringing of the door-bell.

He started and passed his hand over his face as if awaking from a dream.

"God bless her!" he whispered, with unsteady lips. "She has forgiven me! It has come late, but I thank Him that it has come at all."

CHAPTER XXII.

A PITIFUL STORY.

JOHN WILTON paid his call at the Waldorf the next afternoon, and was greeted in the most cordial manner by the man who had once cherished almost murderous thoughts in his heart toward him.

The clasp of their hands, as they met, told each that the bitterness of the past was buried forever—annihilated, in fact; and as they talked over the various incidents relating to their trouble, both felt that— even though they had been the tools of a cunning, designing woman—they needed to be forgiven for much that appertained to it.

Margaret had very little to say, but she sat listening with shining eyes and a look of peace and joy on her face that was good to see after the careworn expression of the past.

Rob and Helen had gone for a drive in the park, and thus there was nothing to hinder their talking everything over with the utmost freedom.

Nothing had so touched Mr. Lancaster in all his life as the story of how John Wilton has relieved the terrible necessity of his wife and daughter by the purchase of their cottage in the Adirondacks, the hiring of their suite, and his fatherly protection of the girl whom they had befriended.

It was an afternoon long to be remembered, and during which old friendships were renewed, and each heart was softened and purified by the acknowledgment of and sorrow for the wrongs of their youth;

while throughout the Lancasters' stay in New York the trio had many friendly and pleasant reunions.

Mr. Lancaster and his party arrived on Friday—having stopped over one day in Chicago on their way.

On Saturday morning that gentleman repaired to his office, making the rounds and shaking hands cordially with each clerk, and inquiring in a friendly way regarding his welfare during his long absence.

When he came to Hubert Alton, the young man flushed hotly, briefly and coldly returning his greeting, then dropped his eyes again upon his work.

During the afternoon, on passing his desk again; Mr. Lancaster paused a moment and said in a low voice:

"Alton, I would like to see you in my private office for a few moments at four o'clock."

"Very well, sir," said Hubert, with a sudden compression of his lips.

He appeared promptly on the notch of the hour designated, and silently took a seat that his employer indicated.

"Alton," began the elder gentleman gravely, and coming to the point at once, "I have asked you to come here to tell you that I feel that I have done you a great wrong. Yes"—as the young man started and flashed a look of astonishment upon him—"I placed a terrible temptation in your way, and I know it is my duty to acknowledge it and ask your pardon for it. Fortunately the—the plan I suggested to you was frustrated, and I find that the sum placed at your disposal in the First National Bank has never been called for."

"Of course not, sir! I had no right to it," cried Alton; but his voice shook, for the loss of that coveted ten thousand dollars had been a terrible blow to him, and had caused him many a sleepless night."

"That is true," said Mr. Lancaster, regarding him

curiously for a moment. Then he added: "I understand that you have recently married the girl who alone should be your wife."

Hubert threw back his head and bravely faced his companion.

"Yes, sir," he replied; "although for a long time I vowed that I never would. I am glad now, however, that I was led to do it, for I know that I should never have taken a moment's comfort if I had carried out my original purpose—even though I might have made millions out of the start you promised to give me. I confess I was fond of Miss Seymour," he went on, paling a trifle. "I had been for years, and I was tremendously jealous of Rob, for I knew that he had the best of me in the race. I know that the only reason why she finally consented to marry me was because she and her mother had reached the bottom of their purse, and she believed it was the only way to save Mrs. Seymour's life. I can see now that we should have been wretched if the marriage had been consummated, and I am glad that it was interrupted, although it was a tough experience at the time. My wife is a good, true little woman, and the better I know her the more sorry I am that I did not do the right thing by her a long time ago."

Mr. Lancaster leaned forward and held out his hand to the young man.

"Alton," he said, "I am more relieved than I can express to find that you have weathered this ordeal so creditably to yourself. I have hated myself ever since I yielded to the temptation that came to me, and then committed a double wrong by tempting you in the way I did. I not only forfeited my own self-respect, but yours also, and I have been fearfully punished. You will understand how severely when I tell you that I have recently discovered that Mrs. Seymour is my wife—from whom a serious misunderstanding separated me many years ago—consequently, Helen is my own daughter."

"Zounds!" cried Alton, almost bounding from his chair at this amazing information, while, knowing of the letter and telegram which had fallen into Helen's possession, he could readily see how complicated matters must have become for Mr. Lancaster. "I never heard of anything to beat that!" he went on, "and you would never have forgiven me if I had succeeded in carrying out your purpose."

"I never should have forgiven myself—I am not sure I ever can, as it is—for having ruined the happiness of my own child and that of Rob, as well," said the gentleman, with a sigh. "I have other news for you, too— they were married a little less than two weeks ago."

"Well, that is news!" exclaimed Hubert, and flushing. "How ever did it come about?"

"Rob and I stopped at Colorado Springs on our way home from Europe, by way of the Pacific, and there met Helen and her mother by accident, the latter having been sent there to recover her strength after her illness," Mr. Lancaster explained.

"Yes, I knew they were there," said Hubert. "Mary —my wife—to whom they were very kind, has written to and heard from them several times."

"Of course, after discovering them, explanations followed, and all misunderstandings were set straight. And now, my young friend," Mr. Lancaster continued, after a moment of thought, "I feel that I owe you some reparation for the wrong I so nearly led you into; full reparation, I know, is beyond my power to make, but from what you have told me, I am sure you will eventually rise above the influence of it, and now, as a proof of my regret, I am going to make over to you that ten thousand dollars that still lies in the First National Bank."

"No, sir! I will not have it!" indignantly exclaimed Alton, as he started to his feet. "It has been too much of a temptation to me already. After I was shown up in my true colors I was even tempted to make the most of that marriage license and draw the money. I told myself it would be easy enough to do it, clear out before I was discovered, and start a good business for myself in some other country. I fought that suggestion of evil as I would fight for my life, and I only conquered it by holding on to the memory of my mother, to whom the commandment—Thou shalt not steal—was about the most sacred one in the decalogue. No, sir; I do not want that money," he continued, more calmly. "I will work for you, and work faithfully, if you will retain me in your service; but if I am ever to rise to financial success it shall not be upon the foundation—pardon me, Mr. Lancaster, but I must say it—of a bribe."

"I deserve that, Alton," said his employer, with a sigh, "and I can but honor you for the stand you have taken—it has lightened my heart more than I can tell you, for it assures me that I have not been the means of corrupting you as much as I feared. But, really, you must let me ease my conscience in some way. Will you allow me to settle the amount upon your wife or child as—as a kind of thank-offering?"

Hubert's face lighted, and he shot a look of gratitude at his companion, in view of this thoughtful proposition.

"Well, Mr. Lancaster, that puts the matter in a somewhat different aspect," he said, after thinking hard for a moment. "If you choose to give it to Mary, I shall be glad for her to have it; only it must be made over to her so that I cannot touch it."

"I will fix that," said the gentleman, smiling at the stipulation, "and now"—rising and holding out his hand again, while he looked kindly into the young man's bright face, "I am sure that you and I will both feel lighter of heart for this talk; we will never speak of the matter again, but we will let it be a lesson to us for all time. You will remain with me as long as you like and continue as faithful to my interests as I am convinced you have been, and your salary is to be increased two hundred dollars per annum."

Hubert gripped the hand he held hard, and then, with a broken "Thank you, Mr. Lancaster," turned abruptly and left the office.

Later, Helen heard something of this interview from Mary, and she was deeply impressed by it.

"He is a good man," she said to herself, and somehow felt as if she had grown a little nearer to her father on account of it.

Mr. Lancaster found business pressing so heavily upon him that he began to fear that he would not be able to get through with it as early as he had planned, and, as he was determined not to keep his wife East until cold weather came upon them, he asked her if she would be willing to attend to a little missionary work for him.

"I should like nothing better, dear," she eagerly responded.

He accordingly gave her a list of his pensioners and of the work that he had laid out for himself, and her face grew luminous with tenderness as she read it over.

"I shall take Helen with me on these visits of love," she secretly resolved, and every day after that for nearly three weeks their carriage might have been seen standing before some humble dwelling in some of the poorer quarters of the city.

What they saw and heard during this time caused Helen to grow more grave and thoughtful than she had ever been before.

Most of the homes they entered were of people who had been rescued from conditions in life that were exceedingly pathetic—many of them even heartrending—but who were now earning a self-respecting livelihood and were proportionately proud of the few steps they had taken on the road to prosperity.

Everywhere Mr. Lancaster's praises were sounded from grateful hearts and lips, and often in a way to cause tears to flow from the eyes of the two women who heard them.

After leaving the last place on the list, where they had found a crippled girl, whose life had been one ceaseless round of suffering until Mr. Lancaster found her out and paid a large sum of money for a critical operation, which had resulted in giving perfect relief to her pain-racked body; and now her expressions of gratitude, love, and reverence for the man were so heartfelt and so pathetically expressed that Helen, on leaving the house, sank into a corner of the carriage and cried as if her heart were breaking.

Mrs. Lancaster did not attempt to check her, for she felt that the lesson which she had meant to teach her when she desired her to accompany her upon these errands of mercy had been most salutary.

On arriving at their hotel Helen sought her own room, and did not appear again until they all met in their private parlor, just previous to going down to dinner.

They were going to the opera that evening, and she had dressed herself all in white and donned her father's wedding-gift—a full set of pearls and diamonds—which gave a touch of brightness and elegance to the otherwise simple costume, while it was a significant fact that this was the first time she had ever worn the costly jewels.

There was a softer expression than usual on her face, a tenderer light in her eyes, while a certain restlessness and nervousness that had been apparent in her manner during the last month had entirely disappeared.

When Mr. Lancaster entered the room she went directly to him and put out both hands to him.

"My father, will you accept your daughter's tenderest love and reverence?" she said, with tremulous lips. "It is a tardy offering, but your conquest is complete."

He caught her to his breast and held her close.

"At last!" he breathed, with something very like a sob. "At last!"

"I have sadly misjudged you," Helen resumed, with her lips lying against his cheek. "I dared to condemn you—to pass sentence upon you, simply because of a few mistakes that you have made during your life—forgive me!"

"But I deserve it all, love—I have merited all the punishment that has been meted out to me," he replied, with a long sigh of mingled regret and relief. Then, looking fondly down into the beautiful brown eyes uplifted to his, he asked, with a smile: "But tell me, dear, what has caused this sudden change in your attitude toward me?"

"Many things," she said, "and for one among the many, I have to-day been to see Annie Capen; yesterday we visited the Wood, Grant and Wells families, and, oh! the good you have done far outweighs all that I have so selfishly judged you for."

"Ah!" said her father, with a swift, fond glance at his wife, "I understand; this is some of your work, dear."

"Well," she replied, the happy tears glittering upon her golden lashes, "I have only helped to prove the prophecy: 'Cast thy bread upon the waters, and it shall return to you after many days.'"

"The days have indeed been long and 'many'; but

I am none the less grateful to have at last won this dear child's coveted love," said the man, as he lifted Helen's flushed, happy face from his breast and pressed a tender kiss upon her lips.

A most enjoyable evening followed, and Helen felt more than repaid for the step she had taken, if in no other way, by seeing the slight cloud that had long shadowed her husband's eyes entirely dissipated.

After five delightful weeks were spent in New York, the party returned to Colorado Springs, where Mr. Lancaster took a handsomely furnished residence not far from the home of Rob and Helen, and settled down with his wife to the enjoyment of domestic life.

The young couple had begged them to come to live with them, but Mr. Lancaster said that no house, however spacious, was large enough for two families; and, besides, he was selfish enough to want his home and his wife all to himself, after being deprived of them for so many years.

Nevertheless, they were a very neighborly quartet, and not a day passed that there was not a most social interchange of hospitalities between them.

Shortly after her return from the East, Helen one day met Marjorie Ellsworth, face to face, upon the street, and she saw at a glance that the girl was looking ill and wretched.

She greeted her kindly, and Marjorie almost broke down as she clasped the friendly hand extended to her.

"What is it, Marjorie?" Helen inquired, "you look almost sick and very unhappy."

"I am," wailed the girl, now utterly overcome. "I wish I were dead!"

"Hush, dear," said Helen, with ready sympathy, then added, as she glanced across the street, "come into the park with me and you shall unburden your heart to me." And, slipping her arm within the girl's, she led her, with gentle authority, into the North Park, opposite which they had been standing, and to a remote seat, where they could talk undisturbed.

She could not bring herself to believe that Marjorie was wholly depraved, in spite of the wrong and deception of which she had been guilty.

"Now," she continued, when they were seated, "pour it all out to me, trust me, for I am still your friend, and will gladly do anything in my power to help you."

"Can you?" said Marjorie tearfully, "after all? For of course you know, now?"

"Yes, I know; but never mind that now. I want to know what is troubling you," Helen gently returned.

"Well, then," began the girl, with an air of desperation, "I have just got to a place where I do not care what becomes of me. Mamma and I have led a cat-and-dog life ever since we came here, and that was bad enough, without the worse things that I have had to meet of late. She is completely soured and changed by our misfortunes, and even though her house is full all the time and she is making money, she has become so avaricious she is all the time trying to overreach people and get the very last penny out of them. She runs in debt wherever she can, and all the tradespeople are finding her out and refuse to trust her; time after time they bring things that she has ordered to the house and take them away again because she is not at home and I have no money to pay for them. Then she never pays the servants if she can help it; she keeps back their wages until they get angry and leave, and then we have to change and break in new ones."

"And doesn't she settle with them when they go?" exclaimed Helen, in dismay.

"No," said Marjorie, "there is always a row, and so she gets out of it. Then, oh! it is horrid to tell you all this, but I am so full I've got to let it out," she interposed wildly, "she contrives to get all the gas we burn out of the boarders. There is a machine in the house—the company put it in because she didn't pay her bills—and we have to put a quarter in every day or we cannot have any light. She waits until it is almost dark, then she goes around and says: "Why! I have forgotten to feed the machine! Will somebody lend me a quarter? I have spent all my change.' Or, perhaps she will show a twenty-dollar bill and ask some one to change it, but of course nobody wants to break it for a quarter, and so somebody hands over the twenty-five cents rather than sit in darkness, and she never remembers to pay it back. The women will sometimes speak of it when they settle; but I suppose the men hate to mention so small a sum and so let it go."

"But I should think they would see through her maneuver after awhile, and no one have any change," said Helen.

"They do, but people are constantly coming and going, and so she manages to keep it up," replied Marjorie; adding, "there are a hundred other things on a par with that, that I can't begin to tell you, and which just mortify me to death. Of course, I can't have any respect for her, neither has any one else; they simply stay with her because the rooms are nice and the board fair. It is a horrid thing to say about one's own mother, but it is disgracefully true. She nags me all the time and then we quarrel. We had a dreadful time on the veranda last night, and of course the neighbors, as well as the people in the house, had the benefit of it, and I wished this morning that I could drop through to China or some other equally remote place. I know that I am disrespectful and people must think me a queer daughter, but I am perfectly wretched to live in such a dishonest way. Mamma tells everybody that she isn't making a dollar, but I know that she is putting money in the bank every week; she is determined to hoard every penny and get out of this kind of life as soon as possible."

"Where is your aunt, Mrs. Sturdyvant?" queried Helen; "cannot you go to live with her?"

"No; Aunt Eliza was suddenly called home several weeks ago, to her sister, who is very ill, and, even if she wanted me, mamma would not let me go. I have to help about the house, you know. But I haven't begun to tell you the worst of my trouble," Marjorie here interposed, with crimson cheeks and heaving bosom.

"Poor child!" said Helen, with gentle sympathy, "well, dear, just empty yourself and perhaps you will feel better, even if I cannot comfort you."

The friendly tone and words were too much for Marjorie's composure, and she broke down utterly, and sobbed for several minutes in an utter abandonment of grief.

"Oh! I do not deserve that you should be so good to me," she said remorsefully, "but I must tell you, for I haven't another friend in this world to whom I can unburden myself."

CHAPTER XXIII.

HELEN'S VICTORY.

"I suppose," she resumed, wiping her streaming eyes after a few moments, "you do not know that I have been—engaged since we came here to live."

"No!" said Helen, in surprise, "although I have seen you driving a good deal with a gentleman."

"That was Dr. Black, the man I expected to marry," returned Marjorie, with a shiver. "He seemed to be very nice when he began to pay me attention, and represented that he had a fine practise, amounting to four hundred dollars a month, and that it was constantly increasing; then some people, whom we knew and who were patients of his, spoke so highly of him we thought he must be all right. Aunt Eliza was pleased when I wrote her about it, and replied that she would furnish a house handsomely for us, as a wedding-gift, and we planned to be married the last of October. After she came, we began to look about for a house, but could not find just what the doctor wanted without paying more rent than she thought we ought, for young people just starting in life; while he also wanted a larger house than she thought advisable to furnish. He was offended because she did not fall in with all his plans, and he began to get sulky and irritable, and show out a disagreeable disposition. He let out things, too, now and then, that made us very uncomfortable. Then auntie began to investigate him, on the quiet, and learned that he did not begin to have as much practise as he had represented, that he was hundreds of dollars in debt, and that his methods were very questionable, if not even criminal in some instances; while his morals and private character were the worst possible. I was frightened when she revealed all this to me. The doctor began to suspect something of the truth, and it made him exceedingly angry. He began to be profane and would swear at me upon the slightest provocation, while I could see that he was often under the influence of liquor—he had worn his mask about as long as he could. I knew that I should lead a wretched life if I married; so I broke the engagement short off."

"You were very wise, Marjorie," said Helen gravely. "I hope you did not really care for him very much."

"No, I know now that I did not; though while he was so nice to me I liked him well enough, and if he had been all that he pretended to be, I believe I should have grown fond of him in time. I—I think I engaged myself to him too hastily," Marjorie went on, flushing violently. "I had known him only a few months, but"—determined to make a clean breast of everything—"when I found that you were here and knew that Mr. Eggleston was going to stop here on the way home and would be sure to meet you, I—I was piqued and I felt that I would like to be married and settled before you made up with each other. I thought, too, it would be nice to have a home of my own."

"Well, Marjorie, dear, you are at least frank in your confidence," Helen observed, a smile of amusement struggling at the corners of her mouth over her confession regarding herself and Rob.

"Well, I meant to be—I am bound to be honest from this time on—if I can," said the girl earnestly. "Well, the doctor was so angry at being turned down, as he expressed it," she resumed, with a heavy sigh, "he swore that he would stop at nothing to be revenged upon me and upon Aunt Eliza, too, for having ferreted him out. He wrote letter after letter to her, filled with the ugliest threats imaginable, together with the falsest and most vicious slander about me, and then began to circulate the same things through the city. Some of these letters he sent through the mail and some by private messenger, until we dreaded to see either the postman or a boy enter the grounds. Auntie kept every one, but never noticed them in any way, until one day she went to a lawyer about the matter. He said at once that the man had been guilty of a State's-prison offense for sending scurrilous matter and threats through the United States mails, and advised her to put the case in the hands of the State inspector and let him put the fellow through. She was just on the point of doing this when she received the telegram calling her home and was obliged to leave on the evening train. I felt as if I had lost my only friend when she went, for I hear that the doctor is still saying the worst possible things about me; he declares that he will ruin my reputation; he has even threatened to shoot me, but I don't believe he'd dare to do that. The last thing I heard, only yesterday, was that he did not really care anything about me, but he knew I was to inherit Aunt Eliza's money, and he was after what he could get in a financial way."

"What a craven!" exclaimed Helen, with curling lips. "Why, Marjorie, he is worthy of only the supremest contempt from every one; and no one, whose opinion is of the slightest account, could fail to despise him for such contemptible conduct."

"Ah, but you know there are always plenty of gossips who are ready to repeat what is said, even if they know the reports are not true, and so I get it from all quarters," said Marjorie disconsolately. "Why, they say the man goes into the various drug stores on the corners, asks a lot of men to drink with him, and then rehearses all the vile things he has said."

"All the same, dear, not one of them believes him and, even though they will listen to him and let him pay for their drinks, they know in their hearts that he is a miserable coward for so attacking a defenseless girl. Where are those letters now?" Helen inquired, after a thoughtful pause.

"I have them locked safely away."

"Well, then, Marjorie, if you do not object, I am going to tell my father, Mr. Lancaster, what you have told me, and I believe he will be glad to espouse your cause and find a way to put an end to such miserable persecution."

"I do not object, and it is very good of you, Helen, to be so interested and sympathetic," Marjorie returned, her great blue eyes full of honest tears of appreciation.

"How does your mother regard the affair?" Helen inquired.

"She is terribly cut up over it, for, of course, in a boarding-house there are always some who are eager to keep the ball rolling, and so she gets fearfully nettled and nags me continually. It seems sometimes as if I should go mad," said the girl passionately, "and I told her the other day that she was getting her pay now for all the wretched things she had said about you and your mother. I never saw mamma cry before, but she got so angry at that that she burst into tears and cried herself into a blinding headache."

"Marjorie! I am afraid you are not very kind to your mother!" said Helen, in a shocked tone.

"How can I be," burst forth the girl excitedly, "when all her life she has been deceitful, dishonest, and full of contemptible tricks that I positively hate? When she had money and life went smoothly with her, she could make people believe she was a lady;

but now she is showing out her true character and it
makes me so ashamed, so miserable. I am sure,
though," she interposed with some asperity, "that you
are the last person on earth I should expect would
defend her!"

"I am sorry for her, dear," was the gentle rejoinder,
"for I know that she must suffer more than any one
else for the wrongs she has done. It is an infallible
law that the evil one does unto others must eventually
recoil upon the perpetrator. It may not appear to be
so in every case, to the world, but the declaration of
the great Teacher—'Whatsoever a man soweth, that
shall he surely reap,' never fails. But," glancing at
her watch, "I shall have to leave you now, Marjorie.
I am glad that I met you and that you have opened
your heart to me, and now I am going to see if something cannot be done to free you from the inhuman
persecution to which you are being subjected. You
shall hear from me very soon." She shook her cordially by the hand, and then they separated.

They were destined to meet earlier than either expected, however, for that same evening, while Helen
was rehearsing Marjorie's story to her husband and
parents, there came an imperative ring of the door-
bell, and a moment later a servant brought Helen a
note and said the messenger would wait for a reply.

Hastily opening the missive, Helen read the follow-
ing·

"DEAR HELEN: I am ashamed to appeal to you, but I
know of no one else to whom I can go in my terrible
extremity. Mamma has been taken alarmingly ill—the
doctor says she has had a shock. She is unconscious
and I overheard the nurse say that she probably will
not live until morning. I am afraid, Helen. Oh!
could you come to me for a little while? Hastily,
"MARJORIE."

There were tears on Helen's lashes when she finished reading the pathetic note.

"Poor girl!" she sighed, and then she read it aloud to her companions.

"Helen, we will go to her at once," said Mrs. Lancaster, as she folded some delicate embroidery upon which she had been working; "that forlorn child must not be left to face such a terrible ordeal alone. You think I am right, do you not, dear?" she added, turning an appealing look upon her husband.

"It is right for you to do just what your kind heart dictates," he responded, as he smiled fondly into her eyes. Then he added regretfully: "I am afraid that my negotiations with Appleton & Wells, for that house they are building, will never be of any benefit to that unfortunate woman. I was intending to ask her this week to look it over and see if it would meet her requirements, and then to give her a deed of it."

"I will go and order the carriage for you while you are getting your wraps on," Rob observed; then he added gravely: "I am sure it is right that we should do everything possible in this emergency, for, however misguided the woman may have been in the past, I cannot forget that I owe my life to her."

Ten minutes later Helen and her mother were on their way down-town, and a little later alighted before the door of Crescent Villa, where they were met and admitted by Marjorie, who threw herself, weeping, into Mrs. Lancaster's arms the moment she saw her.

"How heavenly of you to come," she sobbed, "how could you, after—after—oh!"—cutting herself short with an instinctive feeling of loyalty to the dying woman above—"I wish I could live my life over! There has always been something within me that wanted to be good, but, somehow, I never could let it govern me."

Mrs. Lancaster folded her close to her motherly breast.

"Hush, my dear," she said softly, for the girl was weeping wildly, "none of us can 'live our lives over,' but when we realize that we have made mistakes we can live aright from that time on. We will not talk more of this now, however. Tell me about your mother and how she came to be stricken so suddenly."

Marjorie threw back her head and a lurid fire leaped into her eyes at this reference to her trouble.

"She went out this afternoon," she began, in low, fierce tones, "and met Dr. Black in the street. He stopped her and railed and sneered at her and vowed that he would drive us both from the city and even pursue us with his revenge wherever we might go. Oh! I never dreamed that there could be such vile, vindictive people in the world," she cried out passionately.

"Never mind him now, Marjorie; go on about your mother, dear," said Mrs. Lancaster soothingly.

"Well, she was terribly excited when she came home; her face was crimson and her eyes had such a strange look, and just before dinner she fell to the floor unconscious. A doctor was sent for and she was put to bed. She lies there, breathing still, but knows nothing and—that man is her murderer!" she concluded, with white lips.

"And he will some time have to meet all the evil that he has done," gravely returned Mrs. Lancaster. "I judge, too, that he will have much to answer for in other ways, for my husband said this evening that he has recently heard a good deal about this questionable young doctor. It seems that his methods are repudiated by all self-respecting physicians in the city, that he has made some very serious professional mistakes of late, and it is said to be only a matter of time when he will have to leave the State to save himself from a term in the penitentiary. But put him out of your thoughts, dear, for it only unnerves you to think about him; and now I want you to take me to your mother."

Marjorie lifted a wondering look to the noble woman who could so bury the past beneath a mantle of sweet charity and go to the bedside of one who had spared no effort to ruin her life.

She made no comment, however, but led the way upstairs, and Mrs. Lancaster knew, as soon as she looked upon her, that Marien Waldbridge would never wrong anybody again upon this plane of existence. An hour later she had ceased to breathe.

Helen and her mother, after consulting with the nurse, who seemed to be a sensible, capable woman, decided to leave her in charge of the house and take Marjorie home with them, the disheartened and weary girl being only too glad to go.

The next morning Mrs. Sturdyvant was telegraphed the fatal news, but replied that her own sister was so low she could not leave her; but that she would come on to Marjorie as soon as she was free to do so.

Mr. Lancaster sent her another message, telling her to give herself no uneasiness, for her niece should be well cared for, and everything done for her late sister-in-law that money and good-will could achieve.

The guests at Crescent Villa had fled like a flock of frightened sheep when the dread enemy entered the household, and had it not been for the kindness of those who had suffered most from the enmity of her who had gone, poor Marjorie would have been left desolate and alone with the dead in the deserted house.

Two days later her mother was laid away and, the simple ceremonies over, Crescent Villa was closed and Marjorie went to Helen, to remain until the arrival of her aunt.

Mr. Lancaster settled all bills and arrears, had Crescent Villa put in prime order against the time of the owner's return, and heaved a sigh of relief when all was done, for it had been a gruesome time for them all.

On looking over Mrs. Ellsworth's effects a couple of bank-books were found, showing deposits of more than a thousand dollars, money that she had put away during the few months of her sojourn in the city.

Marjorie was greatly disturbed upon making this discovery.

"I do not want it," she said passionately. "I am ashamed to have it!"

But after thinking that matter over more calmly, she quietly looked up the various servants who had lived with her mother and paid off all arrears with interest. The remainder of the money Mr. Lancaster advised her to let lie in the banks, saying that no one would begrudge her the small amount, even if some of it had been gained by questionable methods.

One morning, on his way down-town, Mr. Lancaster was stopped in the street by a man who was riding in an open buggy, and whom he did not remember ever having seen before.

"Mr. Lancaster, I believe," said the stranger, lifting his hat in a courteous manner, while he smiled blandly.

"Yes, sir, that is my name," replied the gentleman. "Whom have I the honor of addressing?"

"My name is Black—Dr. Black," and he presented his card with a flourish. "Ahem! I understand that Miss Ellsworth is stopping with your daughter, Mrs. Eggleston?"

"Yes. Well!" and Mr. Lancaster's dark eyes began to gleam with a dangerous light.

"Well, Mr. Lancaster, of course you and your family are strangers to me," the doctor continued, but with a wavering glance, "but I thought I would give you a word of warning. Miss Ellsworth is a girl of very disreputable character, and I am sure your daughter's good name will suffer if she——"

"That will do, if you please, sir," Mr. Lancaster here interrupted in a terrible voice, while he drew his splendid figure erect and looked the craven straight in the face, "I have heard of you and of what you are doing to injure the reputation of an innocent girl. I am glad to meet you and have the opportunity to tell you to your face my opinion of you. Do you presume to call yourself a man, or pretend to possess one spark of honor, and persecute a defenseless girl in so vile a manner? Sir, you are a cur, and every decent person to whom you voice your corrupt thoughts and contemptible insinuations would so regard you. And now let we warn you that Miss Ellsworth is under the protection of those who will not allow her to suffer further from your evil designs and persecutions. If I learn of another word of calumny from your lips, I will have you put where you will have to look out of a grated window for some years to come. Those vile letters are in my possession; you have committed a crime against the United States by sending them through the mails, and, upon the very next provocation, they will go into the hands of a United States inspector."

As he ceased he tossed the man's card upon the seat of the buggy beside him, turned abruptly from him, and passed on; while the wilted follower of Esculapius, feeling very much like a whipped "cur," drove away with bowed head and a face that was absolutely colorless from mingled fear, rage, and shame.

It may as well be stated here that his career as a physician was a short one, at least in Colorado Springs; for not long afterward he lost a patient under peculiar circumstances and, fearful of being ar-

raigned for malpractice, he suddenly disappeared, and
it was afterward learned that he had had similar
experiences in other localities.

For three months Marjorie remained with Helen,
and she often asserted that during all her life she
had never enjoyed such a season of content and peace.

Both Helen and her mother felt that there were
many noble qualities in the girl, and which needed
only right conditions and influences to bring them
to the surface, and make a useful and happy woman
of her.

At the end of three months Mrs. Sturdyvant came
for her and, after a short sojourn in the city, took
her back with her to her Eastern home, where, a
year later, Marjorie married a worthy and rising lawyer of New York City, and became the happy mistress
of a lovely home.

She exchanged frequent visits with the Egglestons
and Lancasters, and always regarded them as her
most valued friends.

John Wilton completed his home for poor working
girls, devoting his money and energies to that noble
work as long as he lived, and left his fortune as a
fund to perpetuate it when he was gone.

He often met the Lancasters, and the most harmonious relations existed between them during the
remainder of their lives.

Hubert Alton became a most exemplary man and
a devoted husband and father. He remained in Mr.
Lancaster's service many years, continuing to rise,
and when that gentleman finally retired from the
business, Alton was admitted as junior partner to
the firm.

Mary, his wife, did not serve as matron to John
Wilton's home. Her husband was not willing she
should assume such heavy cares; but she was always

deeply interested in the work, and many a poor girl found her a kind and sympathizing friend.

Rob became enthusiastic in the development of mines and the reduction of ores, developing into a most capable business man and, in time, a wealthy one.

After Mr. Lancaster retired from business he built himself an elegant residence in Colorado Springs, for he and his family had learned to dearly love that land of almost perpetual sunshine, with its loftly mountains, grand scenic effects, and delightful climate. His noble wife and beautiful daughter became very popular; they were loved and respected by every one who knew them, and their homes became the rendezvous of people noted for culture and refinement. And thus the evening of Halburton Lancaster's life was brightened by the sunshine of prosperity and peace and content, while the shadows of his unhappy past and of his great temptation were dissipated and finally obliterated.

THE END

Popular Copyright Books
AT MODERATE PRICES

Any of the following titles can be bought of your bookseller at the price you paid for this volume

Alternative, The. By George Barr McCutcheon.
Angel of Forgiveness, The. By Rosa N. Carey.
Angel of Pain, The. By E. F. Benson.
Annals of Ann, The. By Kate Trimble Sharber.
Battle Ground, The. By Ellen Glasgow.
Beau Brocade. By Baroness Orczy.
Beechy. By Bettina Von Hutten.
Bella Donna. By Robert Hichens.
Betrayal, The. By E. Phillips Oppenheim.
Bill Toppers, The. By Andre Castaigne.
Butterfly Man, The. By George Barr McCutcheon.
Cab No. 44. By R. F. Foster.
Calling of Dan Matthews, The. By Harold Bell Wright.
Cape Cod Stories. By Joseph C. Lincoln.
Challoners, The By E. F. Benson.
City of Six, The. By C. L. Canfield.
Conspirators, The By Robert W. Chambers.
Dan Merrithew. By Lawrence Perry.
Day of the Dog, The. By George Barr McCutcheon.
Depot Master, The. By Joseph C. Lincoln.
Derelicts. By William J. Locke.
Diamonds Cut Paste. By Agnes & Egerton Castle.
Early Bird, The. By George Randolph Chester.
Eleventh Hour, The. By David Potter.
Elizabeth in Rugen. By the author of Elizabeth and Her German Garden.
Flying Mercury, The. By Eleanor M. Ingram.
Gentleman, The. By Alfred Ollivant.
Girl Who Won, The. By Beth Ellis.
Going Some. By Rex Beach.
Hidden Water. By Dane Coolidge.
Honor of the Big Snows, The. By James Oliver Curwood.
Hopalong Cassidy. By Clarence E. Mulford.
House of the Whispering Pines, The. By Anna Katherine Green.
Imprudence of Prue, The. By Sophie Fisher.

Popular Copyright Books
AT MODERATE PRICES

Any of the following titles can be bought of your bookseller at the price you paid for this volume

In the Service of the Princess. By Henry C. Rowland.
Island of Regeneration, The. By Cyrus Townsend Brady.
Lady of Big Shanty, The. By Berkeley F. Smith.
Lady Merton, Colonist. By Mrs. Humphrey Ward.
Lord Loveland Discovers America. By C. N. & A. M. Williamson.
Love the Judge. By Wymond Carey.
Man Outside, The. By Wyndham Martyn.
Marriage of Theodora, The. By Molly Elliott Seawell.
My Brother's Keeper. By Charles Tenny Jackson.
My Lady of the South. By Randall Parrish.
Paternoster Ruby, The. By Charles Edmonds Walk.
Politician, The. By Edith Huntington Mason.
Pool of Flame, The. By Louis Joseph Vance.
Poppy. By Cynthia Stockley.
Redemption of Kenneth Galt, The. By Will N. Harben.
Rejuvenation of Aunt Mary, The. By Anna Warner.
Road to Providence, The. By Maria Thompson Davies.
Romance of a Plain Man, The. By Ellen Glasgow.
Running Fight, The. By Wm. Hamilton Osborne.
Septimus. By William J. Locke.
Silver Horde, The. By Rex Beach.
Spirit Trail, The. By Kate & Virgil D. Boyles.
Stanton Wins. By Eleanor M. Ingram.
Stolen Singer, The. By Martha Bellinger.
Three Brothers, The. By Eden Phillpotts.
Thurston of Orchard Valley. By Harold Bindloss.
Title Market, The. By Emily Post.
Vigilante Girl, A. By Jerome Hart.
Village of Vagabonds, A. By F. Berkeley Smith.
Wanted—A Chaperon. By Paul Leicester Ford.
Wanted: A Matchmaker. By Paul Leicester Ford.
Watchers of the Plains, The. By Ridgwell Cullum.
White Sister, The. By Marion Crawford.
Window at the White Cat, The. By Mary Roberts Rhinehart.
Woman in Question, The. By John Reed Scott.

CPSIA information can be obtained at www.ICGtesting.com
Printed in the USA
LVOW06*0840220414

382711LV00004B/32/P